DAVID R. HUNTER

Christian Education
as Engagement

THE Seabury Press   NEW YORK

Printed in the United States of America

Fourth Printing
414-668-Hl-8-2

ACKNOWLEDGMENTS

The author is deeply indebted to the trustees and faculty of the Episcopal Theological School, Cambridge, Massachusetts, for the invitation to deliver the first Bradner Lectures, which are Chapters 1-5 in this book.

Portions of the lectures were also delivered at the World Institute on Christian Education in Belfast in the summer of 1962, and at the Annual Meeting of the Division of Christian Education, National Council of Churches, in February, 1963. Articles extracted in whole or in part from these lectures have appeared in *Christian Education FINDINGS, Religious Education* (the Journal of the Religious Education Association), and *World Christian Education* (the Journal of the World Council of Christian Education).

Lester Bradner
Presbyter and Teacher
1867-1929

Lester Bradner, in whose memory these lectures were given, was one of the architects of the first large-scale curriculum development project in the Episcopal Church —the Christian Nurture Series. For seven years he had served as director of the Department of Parochial Education in the old General Board of Religious Education, where he was the associate of Dr. William Gardner, the executive of the Board; and he continued in that relationship in the new Department of Religious Education created at the time the National Council was organized in 1919, until poor health forced his resignation in 1924. After a long convalescence Dr. Bradner then devoted the last four years of his life to serving as Field Secretary of Religious Education in the Diocese of Rhode Island and to teaching. Lester Bradner was a Biblical scholar, and he had kept abreast of that field sufficiently to be able to teach Hebrew at Brown University during these closing years.

A former associate of Dr. Bradner speaks of him as "a hard worker, enormously faithful, endlessly painstaking." A gentle, quiet, reflective person, he had an orderly mind and believed in living by the established

order both of the universe and of the society of which
he was a part. Dr. John W. Suter, the Custodian of the
Book of Common Prayer, who became the director of
the Department of Christian Education one year after
Dr. Bradner left the Department, provides an interesting
anecdote about Bradner's sense of order. The two of
them had been working feverishly in New York on a
project, and the next day was to be Columbus Day, a
holiday. As the day ended, Suter suggested that they
next meet on Columbus Day. Bradner refused; Suter
asked why. Bradner's answer was that he deemed it immoral to work on a holiday. He explained that the purpose of holidays was to provide respite and to reduce the
total amount of work done in the course of any given
year. He believed this was a good purpose, and he didn't
propose ever to fail to observe so wise a system—and
he didn't.

Dr. Bradner's four children respected him greatly both
as father and man. To perpetuate his memory and to
further the cause to which he gave the major strength of
his years, they have founded the Lester Bradner Lectures,
a lectureship which will be shared by the Episcopal Theological School, Cambridge, The Protestant Episcopal
Theological Seminary in Virginia, and The General
Theological Seminary, New York City. In this book are
the inaugural lectures of that foundation, and it is the lec-
turer's modest hope that they do honor to the man who
worked hard and wisely in the field of Christian education, knowing its great importance long before others
were ready to respond with the same wholehearted dedi-
cation.

Contents

Introduction

The key word in the approach to Christian education which this book sets forth is *engagement*—meeting, knowing (*not* knowing about), responding to or ignoring, loving, hating. As we use the term, it refers to the experience we are having or ought to be having as Christians: namely, our changing and unchanging encounter with God, our response to His action; or if we are not conscious of encounter with God, it refers simply to God's confrontation of us.

As a theological term, then, *engagement* is the moment when God acts in or upon the life of an individual and the individual faces the obligation to respond. In as much as God is always acting in all life and upon His entire creation, the whole range of one's experience has this theological dimension of engagement. Moreover, since we know from Christian revelation that all experience of this dimension is made possible by God's grace, then the term, in its Christian context, includes the prior action of being met by, being known, being loved by God.

Some may perhaps question our introducing into the field of Christian education the term *engagement*. Our reason for doing so is that we believe it not unfair to say that education today within the Church is not focused on immediate encounter with God; that it is centered, rather, on instruction, on teaching about someone else's encounter. Or to put it with greater theological precision, it is centered on truth, but not on grace,

7

whereas the Word incarnate is full "of grace and truth," and this Word confronts us. Since, then, confrontation is not the central objective of education, there is no term in Christian education which brings into central focus this complex of purpose and experience. It is our hope that the term *engagement* will supply this important, but currently lacking, emphasis.

Dialogue might have been used instead, particularly in view of the enrichment of that term in the thought of Martin Buber and others. It was felt, however, that *dialogue* has the disadvantage of certain associations which might obstruct for some people their grasping the simple, universal fact of encounter with God anywhere, through any person or any thing. Engagement, on the other hand, is a comparatively neutral term in theological semantics and is germane to the central focus confrontation must occupy.

The word *detachment* is used as the opposite of *engagement*. Contrary to the meaning it has in monastic life where it refers to separation from the claims and the demands of the world, here it connotes separation from any conscious sense of confronting the living God and dealing with His action in life. You and I have a way of approaching every issue of life by freezing and objectifying it, by removing ourselves from it, by turning a living demand into a proposition. *Engagement* is the uniting, the reconciling action of God in which we may be caught up. *Detachment* is the separating, fragmenting action of man by which we try to shield ourselves from the pervasive activity of God.

Despite the developments of the last two decades, it is still necessary to state explicitly that the term *Christian education* does not refer only to the one hour program with children on Sunday morning. Rather it refers to the inclusive program designed to provide nurture and training for every baptized person in the Church and having implications for the surrounding community. The extension of Christian nurture and training beyond the Sunday school reflects the growing theological awareness of both the community's and the individual's continuing need for help.

While the word *training* is defined in Chapter 4, an understanding of the sense in which it is used is needed elsewhere in the book. Training refers to more than preparation in the broad sense. It implies "being prepared by becoming involved in." Training implies a kind of preparation for the teaching task that will enable the teacher to encounter the religious issues which are the object of the teaching. In this sense, training has something in common with practice teaching, although it can also take place within certain laboratory and workshop settings.

Another term that needs at least a preliminary definition is the phrase *religious issue*. As used here it refers to any issue which is the consequence of engagement. A religious issue comes into being as a result of a situation where God has acted and man has responded or failed to respond. It is the consequence of engagement and is, therefore, the focus of Christian education.

This book will make occasional reference to the concept of the *Church* as the Church *gathered* and the Church *scattered,* and the approach to Christian education in every chapter relies upon this concept. In our time the World Council of Churches has been an active force in calling us back to a recognition of the fact that the Church, while it remains one Church, has two operating areas. It was gathered together by our Lord, and it continues to be gathered together to receive the sacraments, to worship, to be nurtured, and to be trained. It was also sent into the world by our Lord to join Him in His mission of reconciliation. It can be helpful to Christian educators to keep these two areas in mind.

Finally, the word *mission* is used here in an inclusive sense to refer to the Christian task in the world. It does not refer exclusively to the work of the full-time missionary engaged in home or overseas missions. The mission in which every Christian is called to join is Christ's mission already being performed in the world.

Occasionally, to illustrate our thesis in various chapters, we draw upon examples from the program of the Department of Christian Education of the Protestant Episcopal Church, the author's primary area of experience in applying the principles enunciated in the opening chapters. It cannot be stated too emphatically that these illustrations are not cited because they are deemed to be totally adequate to the situation. Indeed, it is our conviction that there are better ways of centering Christian education upon engagement than those we have thus far employed. Yet it is hoped that the illustrations provided will become the stimulus for the development of more effective approaches.

In the development both of the foundations of this program in the Episcopal Church and of the procedures which have been used, the author shares responsibility with scores of colleagues who have worked with him on the national staff and with hundreds of others who have counseled and assisted us in many ways. The author alone, however, is accountable for the particular articulation which the program takes in this book.

1

The Inescapable Choices
of Christian Education

Christian Education and, for that matter, all education in our day is characterized by three inescapable decisions which every educator makes. These decisions are not so much either-or choices as they are choices of emphasis. In each instance, however, the degree of emphasis may become so decisive as to amount virtually to an either-or choice. The decisions to be made are:

1. Whether to emphasize the aspect of preparation of individuals for the future as against that of ministering to them where they are now.

2. Whether to make paramount the transmission of culture as against stressing the development of the individual as a culture-change agent.

3. Whether to develop a motivation that is dangerously close to being Pelagian (man-dependent) as against one which is a grace-dependent response.

It is not an oversimplification to say that both the field of general education and that of Christian education are almost always given to making the first choice of emphasis in each instance. Education, whether in the name of the Church or society, is usually centered predominantly upon the preparation of people for something which they will do or carry out at a later date, and it

11

attempts to prepare them by bearing down on the transmission of its culture. The Church, often little less than
society, is also essentially Pelagian in the pattern of dependency that emerges from its educational program.

It is the purpose of this book to examine these choices
in the light of Christian theology, particularly the doctrine
of the Church, and to deal with some of their practical
implications for the functions of Christian education in
our day.

The Future vs. the Present

The choice of emphasis between preparing people for
the future and ministering to them where they are now
has been so consistently made in one way that it can be
argued there has been no awareness of choice whatsoever.

Education in our time and throughout most of its development in the West has usually been thought of prin-
cipally as a preparation for the future. A child is prepared
for the next grade, for admission to higher education in
college or university, for a vocation or for a job as a
means of maintaining a livelihood. Of course, a person
cannot be prepared for anything unless the preparation
is related in some way to the present condition of the
learner, and sometimes that present condition has to be
changed if the learner is to respond. In this sense no
"training school" can train without paying some attention
to the present developmental needs of the learner. But
certainly even to state the situation this way is to make
very clear which objective has priority in importance.

The voice of those who would change the priority and
make basic the present needs of the learner is always

heard, but despite several dramatic attempts at change, this point of view has never really gained the ascendancy in American education. The "child-centered" educational program of the 1920's and 30's dominated certain school systems of the country and left its permanent imprint on the entire educational structure of the United States, but it never succeeded in making American education primarily a nurturing medium and secondarily a preparation for the future.

Even if a philosophical case could have been made for an essentially child-centered program, the whole culture of the West would have had to change to make a place for it. In a rising industrial and technological age, which had long since put behind it any pretensions of acquiring goodness for the sake of goodness, or learning for the sake of learning, the focus was always on a task or an urgent need which stood in the future. If anyone was dissatisfied with that approach, what he had to seek to change was not the educational system, but rather the very structure and ethos of society. Granted, one can argue that the structure and ethos of society cannot be changed unless the educational program undergirding the culture is part of the change process. But fundamentally an educational system is the creature of society, not vice versa. It is a means to an end, and the end is not determined by the means, but rather is a part of the given, whether given by society or given by God. A recent illustration of this was the pressure brought upon education in the post-sputnik era to give its major emphasis to science. What society wants in education it usually gets in the long run.

Living in the midst of this kind of culture, it is not

surprising that the Church should be affected by it in determining the nature of its own educational program. The influence is unmistakably clear from the middle of the last century on, the very period when the Church was giving itself to developing an organized educational program, first, for its children, and then, for young people and adults. Previously, the Church had been the initial and dominant force in founding colleges, but even then it had restricted itself largely to training for the future—the preparation of men for the Christian ministry. When it came to providing religious instruction for the young, the developing Sunday school movement became predominantly a process of teaching children the faith for use at a later date. Catechetical instruction was never intended to change or affect the religious situation of the learner immediately. Rather, it was intended to provide a storehouse of values and knowledge for use five and ten years later and throughout the remainder of life.

It cannot be denied, of course, that any form of teaching, catechetical or not, whether meant to be applied one year later or fifty years later, has some effect upon the immediate, developing life of the learner. The subject matter which is assimilated becomes a part of the immediate experience of a child and has some effect on the ongoing, ever-changing value system of the child. Even when a child cannot understand the true meaning of many of the words used in a catechetical answer, he is still bound to vest them with some meaning of his own, and this meaning will join the thousands of other forces that are molding his character, for better or for worse. But certainly these effects, even when positive and desirable, are but a by-product of the main thrust, except possibly when the by-product is so intensely negative as to vitiate and block in later years the coming to fruition of the program's true objective.

Down through the years of the last century there were voices raised against the Church's readiness to conform to the educational patterns of its culture. The first of these, and still one of the noblest, was that of Horace Bushnell, whose monumental book *Christian Nurture,* published over one hundred years ago, is still sound reading for anyone who would have his Church's educational program carry the stamp of the Church's gospel rather than the imprint of culture.

Ponder these quotations from Bushnell's classic:

It is to be expected that Christian education will radically differ from that which is not Christian.

This is the very idea of Christian education, that it begins with nurture or cultivation.

It is the only true idea of Christian education that the child is to grow up in the life of the parent and be a Christian in principle from his earliest years.

No truth is really taught by words, or interpreted by intellectual and logical methods; truth must be lived into meaning, before it can be truly known.

In expressing these ideas, Bushnell was at least fifty years before his time. It was more than half a century later before leaders from one denomination after another slowly began saying much the same thing and in one way or another giving it some kind of tangible form. Bushnell's great emphasis was placed upon the function of the family in Christian education, but even a century ago he saw the need for a parish-wide program of Christian education which would become an integral part of the life and function of the parish church.

Fundamentally, the parish church is not a university or a secondary or an elementary school. As Bushnell clearly saw, it is a source of nurture for persons' souls. A parish church may organize a formal day school, but its principal task is the nurture of souls, since the Christian religion is fundamentally a means of encountering God now, at every age-level, in every moment of our existence. If the parish educational program is not centered on this encounter, then in effect it becomes more an adjunct of society than of the Church. In this sense, *engagement* is both the work area and the goal.

The Christian religion is not primarily a preparation for the future, either in this life or in the next. This is a part of its function, but it is a part which can best be served by giving one's self to Christianity's main function, the encounter with almighty God now.

The espousal of this point of view as it relates to education, however, has until very recent years been left largely to certain leaders within the denominations. The bulk of the Church continued to demand a church school and parish church program based solidly on the tradition of general education and aimed at instructing children primarily as a preparation for their later years. Consequently, even the curriculum materials produced by leaders who saw the need for a change had to remain essentially geared to subject matter, or detached learning, while perhaps containing a certain new degree of option in the area of immediate Christian nurture. An example of the Church's ambivalence on this matter is to be seen in two conflicting statements with reference to purpose which appear in one and the same curriculum. The materials in this church school curriculum were undergirded by the "conviction that the Sunday school must become more than a Bible school or a school for the promotion of certain religious methods inherited from the past. It must place the child first, recognizing his religious nature. . . ." Yet this same curriculum had its eyes on the future more than the present, for it stated that its function was to "set before the Sunday school teacher the task of making his scholars into Churchmen—that is, Christian men and women in action."

The defenders and opponents of most curriculum materials will differ on whether any given curriculum gives adequate attention to the immediate Christian nurture of the child, and it is only rarely that any curriculum states clearly and unequivocally that the emphasis must be on the present. It can still be said that the Church continues to conform to society's insistence that education be geared to relatively long-term goals. The concept of God at work now in the lives of men has not served as a dynamic concept for the educator.

Culture Transmission vs. Culture Change

The second choice of emphasis is between making paramount the task of transmitting culture and enabling a person to become a part of the Christian process which changes culture. In contrasting "culture transmission" with "culture change" we are vesting the word *culture* with two meanings, neither of them strictly identifiable with traditional usage in anthropology. There is the culture or cultus which any group must transmit, and there is also the dominant way of the world in which the cult exists and which exerts influence on the cult and is influenced, in turn, by it.

Every society and community of people, whether religious or not, must take seriously the necessity it faces to transmit its heritage to its young. If it does not do so, it will wither away and die. This is one of our most primitive instincts, with its manifestation to be found wherever people have known corporateness and achieved some degree of national or group identity. The Mosaic admonition to the people of Israel to remind their children constantly that they "were Pharaoh's bondsmen in Egypt" continues to find its place at the very heart of Jewish ceremonial to this present day.

Christianity, too, has a deep and important heritage to transmit. The mighty acts of God down through the ages are fundamental to an understanding of God's actions today, but the Christian religion does not exist *primarily* to perpetuate itself as a religion. It does not exist on earth *primarily* to nurture and keep alive its own life and identity. These things it must do, but it has a purpose and a vocation and *raison d'être* which go far beyond its own self-preservation. It has the task of overcoming the world in which it lives and of which it is a part. In addition to being the transmitter of a culture, it has been given the task of changing culture. This is its mission throughout the world.

This mission, when it is conceived of at all, can be viewed and often is viewed as something that will take place in the future for which we must prepare now. Some would contend that there is a certain logic to this viewpoint, particularly as related to children. We find, however, this same viewpoint prominent in programs for the training of adults. They, too, are trained for a mission to be carried out next year, usually in some other part of the world.

The fallacy and inconsistency of this limited understanding of carrying out Christ's mission in the world is to be seen in the fact that all of us—men, women, and children—are living precisely in the middle of the world all the time. The culture of the West is not a Judaeo-Christian culture, either philosophically, metaphysically, or ethically; rather it is an individualistic, positivistic, materialistic culture, the same culture that dominates the marketplace, the tearoom, the cocktail hour, and the playground. Every time children or adults step forth to encounter another human being, unless they are in the act of worship before almighty God, the chances are that they are then an active part of the world which it is the Church's task to overcome. In these moments of interaction the Christian is either a member of the world or he is a member of Christ's flock. Every Christian, of course, has dual citizenship in these two realms all of the time, but in his behavior at any one moment he is conforming essentially to the demands of his citizenship in the one or in the other. Also, in every moment of interaction he is some kind of a change agent. Either he is contributing to the further watering down of the Christian way of life (which goes far beyond morals), or he is enabling the power of God through his life to affect and change an essentially godless culture.

When, in the Episcopal Church, a child is baptized, he is signed with the sign of the Cross "in token that *hereafter* he shall not be ashamed to confess the faith of Christ crucified, and manfully to fight under his banner, against sin, the world, and the devil. . . ." Any program of

Christian education, therefore, must make up its mind whether it is going to squeeze the theological life out of this statement by stretching the word *hereafter* to mean after so many years, or whether it is going to relate itself to the immediate task of enabling this child so soon as he is able to have interaction with his peers to become a change agent for Christ rather than to be washed along in the stream of culture. Childhood and youth-group culture can, of course, be affected to a degree by adults, but decisive change comes only at the hands of peers. A teenager is much more susceptible to the teenage norm than he is to any standards advocated by his elders.

The record of the churches here is fairly clear and consistent: Christian education for children, young people, and adults is almost solely given to transmitting the heritage and culture of the Christian fellowship. Its focus is on immediate *detachment,* at best future engagement. The careful training of adults for carrying out the Church's mission precisely where they are in relation to the problems of everyday existence rarely takes place; in work with children and youth, it is essentially nonexistent.

Pelagianism vs. Grace Dependency

The third choice is a dependency choice, one which pertains to what we believe to be the source of our ability to do things.

Probably every Christian minister, and most laymen who have studied Church history, have at least a nominal awareness of the Pelagian heresy, but not everyone is quick to recognize it as an ever-present heresy in modern life. The idea that man can lift himself up by his own bootstraps, that he can be the captain of his own soul, that he is so filled with latent goodness and strength that he can do all things through himself if only his will and determination are strong enough—these ideas are contemporary secular manifestations of Pelagianism that go far beyond anything Pelagius himself ever espoused. Yet within the Church—and Pelagius, too, was very much within the Church, at least until his excommunication —there is a constant pressure or tendency to emphasize the importance of man's will at the expense of the priority of God's grace. The resulting tension between grace and free will, between faith and works, is a part of the essential nature and paradox of the Christian life. This tension arises out of the fundamental difference between mortal, sinful man and infinite, loving God; and it becomes actualized when any form of interaction between God and man takes place. Yet despite the fact of this essential tension, one does not have to go to the Calvinistic extreme of double predestination or even embrace Augustine's doctrine of election in order to insist that man is dependent upon both the grace which God gives freely to all men and the sanctifying grace which is ours through the sacraments for the accomplishment of good works. To believe otherwise is contrary to the very drama and process of existence in which every man participates, with or without being aware of it, and which has been enacted for us for all time by God's interaction with man through the life and death and resurrection of Jesus Christ.

Yet, what we do in the name of Christian education often encourages and promulgates, under the protective symbols of the Christian tradition, a motivation which comes dangerously close to being a modern, insidious form of Pelagianism.

Needless to say, one does not come upon blatant ex-

pressions of Pelagianism in materials prepared for use in
the Episcopal Church or in any other Trinitarian communion. This is not the way the heresy expresses itself
and, indeed, it was precisely this fact that caused some
people to be so wrought up about the notorious Pelagius
in the fifth century. Any body of teaching, however,
which in a variety of ways is constantly invoking law, forever appealing to the will, produces results that are more
to be feared than acknowledged atheism itself. Note the
following excerpt from materials currently in use:

> The choices one makes determine the kind of person one
> becomes. Ours is the task of helping to guide our pupils
> to make Christian choices. Ours is the task of guiding not
> only the intellect and the emotions of those whom we teach
> but also the *will to action*. Christian convictions must be
> taught and learned and accepted as one's own. Christian
> courage in terms of God's love and power must be inspired.
> These will lead to definite choices through the changing
> process called Christian education. As Church School
> teachers, we share through Christ in that process of change.

Now these words of advice to the teacher are coupled
with other advice relative to seeking after God's purpose
and the help of God in Christian growth, but the appeal to
will and the appeal to God are separate operations. And
the accent throughout is definitely on training the will to
act. One has to choose between putting the accent on the
will and on the need for grace.

An illustration of the latter emphasis is to be seen in
the following excerpt from current church school materials:

> Grace is God's power, and it is given to man to be used
> in God's way. All of us need and want the power—the

grace of God in our lives. Wherever we may be on the road toward becoming mature Christians, the need for more power to act is always present. This is especially true when we need power to carry out some decision that may have been made when we were "all steamed up." When the steam is gone, we have to ask, "What shall I do?" Working out the answer to this question might go something like this: I can pray to God that I be given power through His Holy Spirit, which I do not seem to have at this moment.

Most church school materials, however, place the dominant emphasis on will. Note the last paragraph of some material which is offered to a teacher for direct transmission to his class either at the primary or lower junior level:

Remember that, when we try to do a hard thing, such as learning to hit a ball with a bat, or learning to skate, we fail lots of times before we finally learn how. So we shall often fail when we try to think of ourselves last, but if we practise and practise, once in a while we may do it. And when we do, we please God very much.

Other quotes from teachers' manuals, picked almost at random, present an appeal to perfectionism which is antithetical to any adequate concept of grace:

Being a follower of Christ means being loyal, courageous, and brave in spite of difficulties.

The pupil must always know that God, through the Church, has provided help for the penitent who has failed to do His will, and joy, with greater responsibility, for the one who has successfully done His will.

Homework also can take on the same spirit:

> Have each one think about the tasks that will be his during
> the coming week and decide upon one, which he does not
> enjoy, that he will try to carry out unusually well, "for His
> sake." Have him write the task on a slip of paper, sign,
> and hand it to you. Remember next week to ask who
> followed through and with what result.

The heresy of depending on will alone, without reference to grace, has ways of creeping into almost everything we do. Even when we do not vest it with words, it
can reveal itself in our attitude. And the prevailing emphasis of a church school can have much to do with determining a young person's attitude about religion. Does
it center in man or in God? Is it chiefly a matter of
morals, of doing what we ought to do—or is it a matter
of looking to God?

The starting point, therefore, in the development of
any program of Christian education is a frank facing of
these three basic choices which everyone makes, willy-
nilly, once he sets his mind at doing something in Christian education. In each instance it is a choice between
engagement and detachment, between living encounter
and some form of postponement or avoidance of encounter. These choices are usually made, knowingly or
unknowingly, when the basic purpose of the program is
framed. The critical moment in the emergence of any
new program is, therefore, the development of a purpose
and objective which will make very clear the three choices
being made and which will, hopefully, be sufficiently clear
and uncompromising to serve as a safeguard against vitiating the choice, once made.

2

The Foundations of Christian Education: Engagement or Detachment?

How does one go about determining the purpose of Christian education? How does one begin? In the Christian Church there is only one beginning, namely God. "In the beginning was the Word, and the Word was with God." When we begin anywhere other than with the priority of God we get into trouble. Indeed, this is the nature of the problem encountered in the three choices educators always face. We can focus our concerns and our purposes on the future as though we were preparing for some distant meeting with almighty God, where in a certain year of our life God will enter and we will be prepared to meet Him. The inescapable fact remains, however, that God is present *now* in our lives. If we put Him first, if He and His action have priority over everything else, then we begin with Him where He is, which is *now* in our lives and in all of His creation.

Then again, we are also given to focusing our objectives on communicating a knowledge of God's actions in the past; but this, too, can be a means of escaping engagement. For if God is really to be found by us, He is to be found in the present, not in the past. He was known in the past, and we can now know about Him in the past, as we must, but we can only encounter Him and know Him ourselves in the present.

And, of course, the choice between man-dependent and grace-dependent response is precisely the choice between beginning with ourselves and beginning with God.

The mission of the Church in all that it does, and therefore the mission of Christian education, is to wait on the ceaseless, ongoing action of the Triune God, as this action calls us forth, with penitent, thankful obedience, to participate in His reconciling work in all creation. The focus must be on what God is doing, not on what we are doing, except as what we are doing is a response to what He has done and is doing. It must be on what God is doing *now,* not primarily on what He has already accomplished in the past or on what He will most certainly bring to pass in the future.

The Areas of Engagement

The two great areas of experience where this reconciling work takes place and where the action of the Triune God can be most frequently encountered are (1) interpersonal relations and (2) the vast social complex of our society. God makes loving demands upon us, and His reconciling work is to be found both in our moral life as we interact with one another and also in our moral life as members of a society and a culture. Our failure to respond to God's action in our life of individual relationships results in the breakdown of these relationships.

Our failure to respond to God's action in our corporate life as a society results in social chaos.

Unfortunately, waiting on the action of God in one of these two areas of our existence does not necessarily mean that we will be cognizant of and responsive to His action in the other. Niebuhr's early book, *Moral Man and Immoral Society,* was one of the first systematic reminders of this fact in modern times. Therefore Christian education has to provide an opportunity for people to explore both areas. The purpose of the exploration in the social area is not to enable us simply to engage in social studies, or to study social problems, or even to become social action enthusiasts. Rather, our objective is to identify the nature of God's action in relation to the social situation and to make possible a response on our part to that action.

Christian education has the task of keeping central the Church's mission as it relates to God's action now, but this is not to say that it can afford to neglect God's past actions or the sure and certain hope of His future action. One means of meeting this situation is to envision the task of Christian education as nothing less than the communication of the Gospel, which Gospel, when it is really communicated, carries with it its own proper balance without any compromise of focus.

The Gospel, which it is the privilege of Christian education and of every Christian to communicate, is the good news that the Triune God has acted, is acting now, and will continue to act in people's lives and throughout all His creation even while He waits and works for our response.

In a general, theoretical way, most Christian educators

would accept this statement, but their means of implementing it would range widely. The problem comes in the balance or the degree of emphasis which should be accorded the three elements: God's past action, His present action, and His future action. All three are indispensable: a knowledge of what God has done in times past is indispensable to an adequate understanding of and response to God's activity in our life and world today; a personal knowledge and recognition of God's presence and action in our life and world today is essential for an adequate comprehension of God's activity in the past; and a sure and certain hope for the future based securely upon God's past and present revelation is necessary if man is to maintain Christian perspective on matters pertaining to existence, time, and eternity. The Gospel cannot be communicated to people solely in terms of God's past action or solely in terms of His present action, much less His future action. A means must be found through which these three elements may be kept in proper, but not necessarily equal, balance. That proportion is proper which best facilitates confrontation of God now, followed by response. Engagement must be the immediate and the ultimate criterion.

The Nature of Religious Learning

But we find many ways of avoiding engagement and of getting around the problem. One can argue with a certain degree of logic that learning always requires a subject-matter base. That is to say, recognition and identification of immediate experience requires a basis on which the recognition and identification can be established, and this basis is found in the symbols provided by man's past experience. Some would contend, therefore, that we should teach subject matter first and help people to deal with their immediate experience later. This kind of reasoning either is unconsciously demonic or becomes quickly susceptible to demonic influences, for the second step is usually so much the victim of postponement that it scarcely ever gets treated with anything approximating the systematic care which is given to unfolding man's past experience.

But even if that were not so, this reasoning ignores the fundamental nature of religious learning, learning that pertains to God's action. God is the source of this learning, and God is an essential force in the operation. For this reason, we cannot possibly understand His mighty acts of old apart from His present revelation of Himself. When the Church engages in education, we are really dealing, therefore, with two sides of a single educational operation. A way must be found whereby, without ignoring the essential nature of each element in the process, we avoid the mistaken notion that one has to come before the other.

Others will insist that the interchange between God and man simply does not apply during the early years. It is claimed that at certain preschool and elementary age levels a child does not have the capacity to understand the presence of God in His own life. Consequently, the task of focusing on God's present action ought to be reserved for later years of greater maturity. Again, the demonic element in this reasoning is at least suggested by the fact that neither adult materials nor courses for junior and senior high school show any greater amount of such focus than is to be found at earlier ages.

The point of view is more than self-delusion, however.

It is heresy to infer that a child is not capable of responding to God's action in his life. There is a difference
between understanding and response. A preschool child
is incapable of understanding most of the things he will
understand in his adolescence, but God is acting in his
life at one age just as certainly as He is at another. Where
understanding is possible it is a necessary ingredient for
Christian learning, but where it is not possible, then other
ingredients suffice. A child, for instance, experiences and
wonderfully benefits from the love he receives from his
mother long before he is able to understand that love.
In those early years before understanding is possible, this
love is not withheld from him, and he is encouraged to
respond to it. We would all find immediately repulsive
a program of child care that carefully segregated children
from their parents except for occasional visits, devoting
the early years to telling children stories about the many
wonderful experiences their parents and grandparents
have had with other people and which they, too, will
sometime have with their parents when they reach maturity. Yet it is not an unfair comparison to say that in the
development of curriculum we adopt that very procedure
as it bears upon a child's relationship with almighty God.
A few fleeting visits with God through teaching the child
to pray are provided, but God's presence in the child's
life apart from these moments of prayer does not find a
place in the program.

In short, the theology of a Christian education program
is determined by what it assumes about God, about the
mission of the Church, and about salvation. It will either
be theistic or essentially deistic, according to the amount
of attention it gives the action of God in the lives of

learners and throughout all creation. Its understanding of the Church and the mission of the Church will be revealed by the degree to which it consciously and persistently provides its people with training in the ongoing, never-ending task of sharing Christ's ministry of reconciliation in the world. Its doctrine of salvation will be either incarnational or essentially Pelagian in character, depending upon the real place of grace and will in the whole warp and woof of the program.

Much depends, therefore, on how seriously one takes the task of establishing the purpose of an educational program. Unless there is a deep conviction that the program must find its focus in what God is doing, and that the Church's task is one of enabling man to respond to what God is doing, the culture of our day will assert its influence and one compromise with the faith after another will follow. Not until Christian education is seen as an integral arm of the mission of the Church, with its roots deeply planted in the theological imperative of the faith, are we likely to withstand the cultural influence. Even then we will slip, and engagement will give way to detachment. For this reason we need all of the built-in barriers to slipping and compromising that we can possibly construct. Actually we need an engagement methodology all our own that is a direct outgrowth of our theological imperative. If we use the traditional methodology of general education, not to mention religious education, we will be under the constant influence of traditional procedures which will make compromise easy. The following chapter considers a methodology for Christian education which is consistent theologically with its objectives.

3

The Methodology of Christian Education: Engagement or Detachment?

Building an educational program is in a very basic sense quite similar to erecting a building, conducting a political campaign, or planning a large-scale military operation. All of these must conform to certain elemental steps of procedure or little will come of the operation. One must, first of all, arrive at an understanding of the situation that gives rise to the need. Second, the real dynamics of this situation, what makes it what it is, must be correctly identified. Third, a strategy for approaching and coming to grips with these dynamic forces must be devised. Finally, the tactics or steps and resources required to carry out this strategy must be planned and procured.

Notice the degree to which each of the last three steps emerges from the one preceding it. Each is in fact determined and made mandatory by the foundations of the whole undertaking—the situation of need that is calling for action. The need for offices or housing leads to a survey of the precise kind of function called for. This gives way to architectural planning which, in turn, determines the nature of the materials required. If any of these steps is omitted, executed mistakenly, or taken irresponsibly, the need will not be met, and eventually someone else must make a new attempt. The history of political economy provides numerous examples of the applicability of this procedure to politics. Among the most obvious in this century in our own country are the political careers and campaigns of those who achieved the presidency. Theodore White's best seller on the presidential campaigns of 1960 is but the latest demonstration of the importance of a strategy that was faithful to all four elements.

Wars cannot be said to be started on any such rational basis, but, once started, they are usually won or lost in precisely the same way.

In education these steps are no less fundamental and essential; but educators, particularly religious educators, have an uncanny way of glossing over or completely omitting the two middle steps. We jump immediately from a comprehension of the general situation to a succession of tactics for doing something about it. The general religious situation is often thought to be that we are living in a time when man knows very little about God and refuses to acknowledge the presence of the supernatural in his common life. So we construct courses to give people a knowledge about God and His activity, usually His mighty acts in the ages which have preceded us. This procedure would appear to be logical enough, but in operation, more often than not, it has been quite irresponsible and illogical because the planners have neglected to identify and take seriously the dynamics of man's failure to know God, and have also neglected to evolve an over-all strategy for relating the educational program to these dynamic forces. We move from general situation to tactics. We refuse to grapple with the real forces that constitute the religious situation. We prefer an impersonal, academic (in this case superficial) approach to a personal, dynamic approach. We prefer that our education be detached from the process of history rather than engaged in it.

It is the purpose of this chapter to deal with the two middle steps and thus to propose a methodology sufficiently comprehensive to permit a faithful response to the demand that is upon us.

Dynamics of the Religious Situation

In a theistic universe any situation is a religious situation, for God does not absent Himself from the objects of His creation. Whether or not we recognize any given situation as religious depends upon our understanding and recognition of God's role in it, although that does not at all affect the fact that the most important aspect of *every* situation and experience of life is the activity of God to be found in it. Either God is acting in the whole of life, or He is not. If He is not, then theism disappears as a viable approach to an understanding of human experience. If He is acting in the whole of life, then there can be no questioning the paramount importance of this fact. In God's action is to be found the central dynamic force of every situation.

There is no real reason for quarreling with the characterization of our religious situation as "a time when man knows very little about God." Much more can be said about our knowledge of and relation to our fellow men and to nature, but basic to these is the inadequacy of our knowledge of God and the supernatural. In short, we do not know the Gospel, the good news that the Triune God *has acted, is acting now,* and *will continue to act* in people's lives.

The dynamic factors in the religious situation are the *religious issues* which come into being when God acts and man responds or fails to respond. Within the dialectic of this divine-human encounter are to be found the religious issues. The symptoms of these religious issues are the joys and sorrows, the doubts and convictions, the reconciliations and separations, the satisfactions or frustrations, the prejudices and passions, and the never-ending succession of viewpoints that characterize our everyday living. Here again, all of the issues of life are fundamentally religious issues. They are the issues brought into being by an initiative taken by God which, more often than not, is not responded to by man. Even when man does respond positively, however, his response is never complete and full. But regardless of the degree of adequacy, our response or the lack of any response creates an occasion which becomes an issue in our living. There are times when this issue is characterized more by joy than by sorrow or fear; but, alas, the reverse is perhaps more often the case.

The religious issue, arising out of the divine-human encounter, is either man's unsolved problem or his unearned joy. In either case it is his best pathway to an enlarging or deepening of his knowledge of the Gospel as the Gospel relates to his own life, for it leads directly to the action of God, the "Hound of Heaven," within our own experience.

It would be quite beyond our power to *know* God in

the sense of comprehending His every action if the initiative rested with us, but it does not. The first step is not
ours. God Himself has taken that first step and the second
and the third. He has revealed and continues to reveal
His own activity in His work as Creator. "The heavens
declare the glory of God." He has revealed and continues
to reveal His action among men and within men through
Jesus Christ, "who for us men and for our salvation came
down from heaven"—"full of grace and truth"—"who
gave himself a ransom for many"—"who is even at the
right hand of God, who also maketh intercession for us."
This same revelation continues to come to us through the
working of the Holy Spirit in the sacraments and in "being
gathered together in unity" within the Church. Most
abundantly this revelation has come and continues to
come to us through the Bible, where we see God in times
past and today engaging in two kinds of action which
are indeed one action. He is constantly making demands
upon His creation and just as constantly offering us His
reconciling love. With unabating faithfulness this action
continues. Whether we care or not, though we be callous
and deaf to His movements, unaffected by our own un-
faithfulness He waits and He works for our response.

And as this drama continues within us, with all of its
consequences filling men's hearts and affecting their
world, God waits and works not only for man's individual
response, but for the response of the whole Body. There
are vast segments of God's people, ourselves among them,
who at any one time will not make their response unless
they are assisted by others. This is the situation of need
for which Christian education exists, and the religious
issues of our everyday life are the dynamic forces at the
heart of that situation.

Organizing Principle

Once we have proceeded this far, the task of determining an over-all approach that will cope with the
real situation is not difficult to come by. It is indeed
prescribed by what has gone before. In education, methodological planning boils down to deciding what the
organizing principle shall be. Around what will the educational course or activity be organized to give it conti-
nuity and sequence? Every curriculum, every course,
and every class or group session needs some kind of
structure that will enable teachers and leaders to move
ahead with sufficient order and relatedness. The choice
of organizing principles is not great. There are only two
choices. The course receives its direction either from
what is happening in the lives of the students or from
what has already happened in the minds of an editorial
board. The choice is between living issues and traditional subject matter.

The organizing principle of most educational programs
in the Church has been subject matter. Living issues have
at times been treated in such a way as to turn them into
quite readily detached subject matter. One partial illustration of the latter is the Character Research Project
developed by Dr. Ernest Ligon and his associates. This
project uses a carefully predetermined sequence of character traits which are studied and nurtured on schedule
over a period of two years. Thus, while a factor with
engagement possibilities, namely, character change, is
the target of the program, the organizing principle is not
character change in the lives of the specific people in a
class but character change according to a schedule created

by the curriculum builders. Character change takes on
the detached characteristics of subject matter, which is
meant to be applied in a standardized fashion with as
much adaptation as possible. The data of this program
reveal that it has a much better chance of connecting
with reality in children's lives than do traditional subject-
matter courses, chiefly because of the nature of the objective, but the organizing principle is still distinctly
detached from the ongoing life situation. A course moves
forward from week to week according to a system-wide
pattern. Only the Holy Spirit could turn an established
system-wide pattern into engagement and, except for the
liturgy, He doesn't seem to choose to do so!

When religious issues are selected as the organizing
principle of a curriculum or educational program a search
begins for the particular manifestations of a given religious issue that are sufficiently common at a given age
or experience level to warrant making preparation for
dealing with them. (Notice that we are talking in terms
of "preparation for dealing with" them rather than "teaching" them. This is the difference between an engagement
approach and a detachment approach. See Chapter 4,
"Engagement Training for Nurture.") After careful
study and experimentation, the curriculum builders make
a selection which determines the broad channels of each
specific course. Examples of these issues in the lives of
children and youth can range from the appreciation of
animals and life (a choice that would be appropriate at
the second-grade level), to the problem of right and
wrong (fourth grade), to the clash of freedom and authority (seventh grade), to decision-making (eleventh
grade). The purpose of a teacher's manual, or leader's
guide, then, becomes severalfold:

1. The teacher must be provided with sufficient assistance in observing and recognizing the manifestations of the kind of religious issue known to be common at that age or experience level. As data accumulate, succeeding revised manuals ought to contain a wide variety of the many ways in which a particular religious issue gains expression or reveals itself. In general, these are the same for all mankind regardless of age, yet they take many different forms. They are the joys and sorrows, disappointments and fulfillments, fears and assurances, doubts and convictions, likes and dislikes, loves and hates, envyings, strivings, desires, and ambitions—each clothed in a form characteristic of its own manifestation in persons of a given age. Once recognized, these manifestations can become the focus around which weekly plans and the year's work may be organized.

2. Untrained and inexperienced teachers must be given help in relating themselves to these manifestations, once recognized, as well as suggestions for eliciting response from the class or group and a willingness to deal with the issue in ways appropriate to the age-level. Precisely the same kind of help is needed in adult education where age-level characteristics largely give way to cultural norms, vocational interests, or common concerns.

3. The manual must also be a handbook for assisting teachers in relating a specific religious issue to the most relevant resources both from the past and from the ongoing life and experience of the congregation. There is no end to the amount of subject matter that can be used profitably in this fashion. It is significant, however, that when a whole book or other large seg-

ment of Biblical material is introduced, it is used not as
an entity in itself but because it is germane to the live
religious issue which is currently in focus.

When religious issues are the organizing principle of
a course, then the many manifestations of the religious
issue around which a particular course is organized become a reservoir to be used as one after another of these
manifestations appears in the current experience of the
class. Sufficient resources and aids must be at hand in
the manual to enable teachers either to follow a particular
approach to an issue for only a session or two, or to
pursue it in depth for several weeks or months. Each
approach must have the possibility of becoming the total
course in microcosm. The extent to which any one approach is used will depend upon the readiness of teacher
and students to stay with it. When this readiness disappears, then the teacher must be helped to move along to
another, perhaps quite different, manifestation of the
same fundamental issue, but always one that has already
been observed in the group. In this fashion religious issues determine the unfolding direction and organization
of the course.

When subject matter is the organizing principle (as-
suming the same purpose in terms of communicating the
living Gospel), the work for a given year is planned and
given direction around a certain body of material such as
Church history or the life of our Lord. Each session or
unit is studied in itself, and then an attempt is made to
relate the message and meaning of the subject matter to
manifestations of religious issues in the current experience
of the group members. When this process has run its

course, the next chapter or unit of subject matter determines where the class goes next, and the cycle repeats itself.

The difference between the two organizing principles is not in the fact that one must always start with a religious issue and the other with subject matter, for in the interest of accomplishing an effective approach the start can be made from either point under either organizing principle. The difference is in terms of strategy planning. The life of the class as observed by the teacher is decisive, in one instance; in the other, the editors determine this vital matter.

On the assumption that teachers can be trained and supervised on a sufficient scale to organize their work around religious issues, a strong case can be made for this method. If the underlying purpose of one's program is to enable people to respond now to what God is now doing in their lives, then the navigator ought to navigate with his eye on what is happening to his craft. A prepared chart cannot possibly show in advance all of the changes in winds and weather or all of the emergencies which will demand on-the-spot decisions.

No Bermuda race has yet been won by a helmsman and crew who changed tack at the time and place a book directed. Fortunately for yacht racing, no such book has ever been written. In Christian education if one's main endeavor is to communicate a certain body of subject matter, then it is appropriate to be guided by the best arrangement of the material that past experience can provide, with due consideration to the response of the class. If immediate response to God's action is the central objective, then the response of the class will be primary, with due consideration to a wise and adequate use of all the Church's resources.

There are those who believe in the purpose of Christian education along engagement lines as expounded in these chapters, but who insist that either organizing principle is usable and will be effective if the purpose is kept clear. The weakness here is in the conditional clause. The purpose is not kept clear when it is not the determining factor at every step of the way. This failure of purpose begins at the level of publication, and it can find its way into every class session. The subject-matter oriented curriculum series which has the greatest use in the Episcopal Church at the present time states its purpose as being "to guide the children in living the Christian life *now,* at their present age, and to furnish their hearts and minds with resources that can be developed in their future life in the Church as young people and adults." Yet, in the opinion of Professor Charles Batten of the Episcopal Theological School, who reviewed this series, "one of the greatest weaknesses of the series is a disparity between the announced and formally stated philosophy and the materials and the methods in the manuals whereby this may be achieved." Little help is provided in enabling the teacher to understand the children at a given age; even less help in relating subject matter to religious issues. In this sense these materials do not differ from any other curriculum materials which use subject matter as the organizing principle. If a course is not really dependent upon religious issues for its development, it is natural that only passing attention will be given to them.

Likewise, when teachers use subject-matter centered materials, they usually tackle the task of communicating this material first, reserving "application" for the latter part of the hour. More often than not, time runs short, and little or no attention is given to religious issues. And then a corrosive effect sets in which gradually causes the stated purpose to disappear. The teacher knows that something of some value has been accomplished in communicating subject matter, and the lack of time to deal decisively with issues or to deal with them at all is dismissed with the feeling, "Well, at least I taught them something." This sense of accomplishment is as common an illustration of educational seduction as can be found anywhere in professional or nonprofessional teaching. It is the classic example of the collapse of purpose under the influence of method.

Of course, it is possible for purpose to win out over method and thereby to transform and change the method. The best teachers one has known have demonstrated this. The most beloved teachers have been those who, as the result of their commitment and their love for their pupils, were forced to put the needs of their pupils first. Although starting with subject-matter centered materials, once they knew the religious situation of their pupils, they felt completely free to depart from their "place" in the prescribed text and go to some other section or even outside the text or manual to find and use what the class needed at the particular moment. Whenever that happened, the teacher was adopting as organizing principle, the religious issue.

In the early experimental prepublication days of the official curriculum of the Episcopal Church, both on grounds of principle and in response to experimental data, the curriculum builders were led to the firm decision that the use of religious issues as the organizing principle

completely ruled out the possibility of providing teachers
with prefabricated lesson plans for each of the Sundays of
the year. Even so, the editors were under pressure to
establish a given sequence of manifestations of religious
issues which could be followed as a study guide throughout the Church; but this would have turned engagement
issues into detached propositions, since religious issues
exist only in the lives of people. Despite heavy demand
for weekly lesson plans and a rival curriculum which
provides these, the official materials for the Episcopal
Church continue to emphasize the necessity of tailor-
made plans by the teaching team on a week-to-week basis.
Educational methodology is dictated by educational purpose. When the methodology deviates from the purpose,
the purpose changes.

Learning Theory

Any treatment of methodology ought to include an
exposition of the learning theory to which a program of
education adheres. How do we understand Christian
learning to take place? In the case of the program of the
Episcopal Church's Department of Christian Education,
it should be made clear that the program is not the result
of the methodological theory, but precisely the reverse.
The theory that emerged from the developing program
was an outgrowth of the basic purpose of that program,
and exists now as a guide in its further development.

Both the occurrence of learning and the integration of
learning depend upon the eventual coalescence of four
elements of experience. While there is some meaning
attached to the order of the four, they do not necessarily

occur in the chronology here indicated, and since the coalescence is never complete, the four elements ideally take on a kind of cyclical order. These four are:

1. Immediate personal encounter
2. Identification of the encounter
3. Symbolization of experience
4. The ordering of experience

In recognizing these four elements we are not identifying anything that is peculiar to religious knowledge or Christian education. We do not learn secular truth one way and religious truth another. Truth is truth, and when it is comprehended and assimilated and understood and used the distinction between sacred and secular falls away. To make this quite clear we will take two examples that have their setting in the area of general learning (which can be just as religious as any formalized educational opportunity fashioned by a church group). One of these illustrations will be (A) that of a child who burns his hand. The other will be (B) of a man who is called upon to cheat in his work.

1. The immediate personal encounter with reality.

    A. A child touches a hot stove and recoils in pain.
    B. A man is confronted with a demand in his work that he engage in misrepresentation.

2. The identification of what is being encountered in relation to some aspect of an issue of life which it manifests. This is a process of reflecting back upon, identifying, and describing what has been experienced.

    A. The child immediately begins to associate the pain and shock with the stove which produced it.

He may begin to associate the pain with the physical sensation produced by heat or warmth. The painful experience takes on identity related to the factors which produced it and to the sensations which accompanied it.

B. The demand to misrepresent causes the man to relate the demand to certain standards of behavior already acquired from other sources. He may also relate the demand to other conflicting demands which are a part of him. The demand takes on some kind of identity, even though the identity may later be suppressed or changed under the pressure of conflict.

3. The relating of immediate experience to the symbolization of past experience.

A. The child relates the experience of heat and pain to the semantic symbol "burn." He may also relate pain from heat to his parental symbol of authority, the parent having already warned him not to touch the stove.

B. The man may relate his conflicting demands in his present situation to his understanding of his mission in the world as a baptized Christian. If he has no understanding of any such mission, then this symbolization of his immediate experience does not take place. Whether he has it or not, it can be supplied and the symbolization is always a possibility.

The man may relate his present conflicting demands with many similar situations in the past and merely accept them as "the way things are."

4. The ordering of what has been encountered in relation to all other learning (by direct experience or by symbol).

   A. The child begins to relate his immediate experience to his growing world, which includes fire in different forms, matches, fire engines; he also relates this experience to pain in other forms. He begins to relate his immediate experience to his enlarging experience with his parents, from whom he needs protection in other ways and whose authority in other matters he must increasingly accept.

   B. The man may integrate his learnings by entering into various kinds of decisive action involving:

      (1) Seeing himself a part of the great company of witnesses who have known the mighty acts of God in every age.

      (2) With all of God's faithful, offering himself and his decision to God at the altar.

      (3) Joining with his fellow Christians in a form of action in the world which is his social response to the demand.

      Or there may be no learning in this particular experience. It may only be a confirmation of past experiences where the conflict has been suppressed.

If we use these four elements of learning in understanding and categorizing the nature of man's response to God, it then becomes possible to say that Christian learning involves an awareness of the action of God within our lives, a recognition of the religious issues which are created by God's action and our response, a relating of this experience and these religious issues to the mighty acts of God in the past, and, finally, some comprehension of the relationship which this experience or symbol has to the whole body of Christian revelation and Christian experience.

It must be remembered that these elements do not necessarily constitute a sequence of learning. It is possible for a learning experience to begin with either the first or the third element, with immediate encounter or with the encountering of a symbol of someone else's experience. The learning is not complete in any appreciable sense until all four elements have become a fact in the experience of the learner.

This example, then, illustrates engagement methodology designed to implement a faith that is centered in engagement and has little to do with detachment. This methodology is in operation to some significant degree in the educational programs of more than twenty-five hundred parishes in the Episcopal Church. It will continue to bring meaningful results in these parishes as long as the faith of the parish and its educational program remain focused on engagement. When engagement gives way to propositions and forms and detached idolatry, then there are less demanding and less rewarding ways of discharging our responsibility to do something in the name of education.

4

Engagement Training for Nurture

In responding to the central purpose of Christian education, the two overarching tasks of Christian educators
are to supply adequate resource materials and to train
leaders. Everything a national board of education does
falls into these two areas, and the same is equally true of
a local church—unless the minister of the local church
insists on doing all of the teaching himself and sees no
need for training anybody else. Even in that case the
minister must submit himself to training.

If the education which is to take place, however, is to
be related to the Christian faith as it is actually being
lived in the parish, no one person can effectively operate
in an educational capacity at all age-levels at the same
time. At best he can do this only through preaching, in
itself no small task; but there needs to be a follow-through
to preaching, and the activity of education is that follow-
through.

Selected individuals, therefore, need to be trained to
assist the minister in providing necessary leadership, and
the word *train* is used here with forethought. *Train* can
be objected to on the ground that animals are trained and

persons are taught, but from the standpoint of the basic
meaning of these words, a case can be made for using
train rather than *teach* or *develop*.

The usual meaning of *teach* is to impart knowledge or
skill, whereas to *train* is to make proficient by instruction
and practice. The difference between the two is not abso-
lute, but it is significant for those who give a central place
to engagement. *Training* definitely involves proficiency
and practice. *Teaching,* while it can denote communicating a skill, is more specifically related to communicating
knowledge about something. Even in making our first approach to the requirements for leadership, there is wisdom
in allowing our semantic choice to be influenced by the
basic objective of Christian education. If our objective
is to help people confront and react to the deepest process
that is at work both in their soul and in their life as a
society, then the concept of training has in it a degree of
activity, of ongoing aliveness, which is not necessarily
explicit in the image of teaching. If we are preparing a
person to do something, it is rather appropriate to think
in terms of training. If we are enabling a person to understand something or to think or to believe something, then
the word *teaching* seems to be in order. Actually, in any
adequate educational program we are doing both, but in
most Christian education, which is usually inadequate,
we attempt to teach and we do little training. As we
indicated earlier, this is due either to an inadequate con-
ception of our task or to our surrender to some lesser task.

In recent years certain churches have substituted the
term "leadership development" for "leadership training."
At first thought this substitution of words would seem to
have certain advantages, but they probably accrue only

if we associate training with animals. Indeed, there can be a profound theological difference between the concept of training and the concept of developing. The core meaning of the verb *develop* is to bring out the capabilities and possibilities of someone. And there is hidden in this terminology at least the seeds of a liberal humanism which presupposes that man has within him the capacity for doing what he ought to do. While the concept of training can have other undesirable theological connotations, at least it does not have this Pelagian tinge.

This chapter will unfold a specific training program of the Department of Christian Education of the Episcopal Church with particular attention to its nature as engagement. This training program constitutes only one effort to put into practice the basic philosophy and theology of Christian education which has already been set forth. The program is an evolving one, far from static, and it is hoped that it will yet take many other forms.

The Department's understanding both of its objective and of the methodology that would be consistent with that objective developed slowly over a period of five or six years. The Department's understanding of its training function in terms of engagement training emerged suddenly in 1953, in the immediate wake of the crystallization of its methodology, and all that has been done since then can be properly classified as engagement training. Looking over the full sweep of these nine years, however, it is clear that two kinds of engagement training have come into being as a result of our growing understanding of the two necessary operating areas of the Church. These are the operating areas of the Church gathered and the Church scattered.

Fundamental to everything contained in this book is the wholehearted conviction that while the Church is one, it has the necessity of living its life and carrying out its work in two distinctly different areas. It is called to be the Holy Fellowship, the worshiping community, the Body of Christ in adoration and in praise, as well as in penitence and in receipt of absolution. But it also exists in the world, at work, doing those things which it must later bring to the altar of God if its life at the altar is to have real meaning. In one sense the Church gathered and the Church scattered is one action, for one might be said to be the origin and the other the fulfillment, but this is so only in the most abstract, theoretical way. In actuality we separate the two quite decisively, even though in many effective ways we achieve relationship between the two. So long as the Church is made up of sinful men—and there is no foreseeable end to that—the Church will probably always have to maintain the rhythm of moving from worship to work and from work to worship.

The Church gathered is the area of the Church's life and work where we receive and enter into the sacraments, where we worship, where we are nurtured in the faith, and where we are trained for work in the world. The Church scattered is the membership of the Church carrying out its mission in the world, the world of daily work, of family living, of recreation and leisure time. This chapter and the next, therefore, will treat two distinctly different types of training operation: the first, training for nurture in the Church gathered; the second, training for mission in the Church scattered.

The American composer, Aaron Copland, once wrote, "You can't develop a better appreciation of music by reading a book about it. If you want to understand music better, you can do nothing more important than listen to it." Whereupon Copland proceeded to write his book. But, even so, his emphasis was sound pedagogically. Books are necessary for any training operation, and part of religious training will certainly pertain to teaching people *about* religion. Yet the heart of the training operation must consist of training them *in* religion.

Orientation Training

In the experience of the Department of Christian Education there are three necessary kinds of training for nurture if the training is to be engagement training. The first of these is orientation, the second procedural, and the third in-service training.

Orientation training enables people to find themselves in the Church, in the Body of Christ, precisely where they are. The average churchman knows himself somewhat as an individual—certainly not entirely, but he knows himself as an individual more than he knows himself as a member of the Church. He knows himself somewhat in relation to his family, somewhat in relation to his community and his nation, somewhat in relation to his work. But the average churchman has only found himself partially in his identity as a churchman.

The average churchman belongs to many groups and institutions. He has a meaningful consciousness of belonging to some of them; his relationship to others is only nominal or legal. His sense of belonging to the Church ought to have a quality different from any other in his daily experience, for this is the institution and group in which the Holy Spirit dwells, wherein God acts to bind us together into one family, through which the grace of God comes to us in the sacraments. If God is acting at all times in our lives, within the Holy Fellowship of the Church He is perhaps acting no more than elsewhere; but He is nonetheless acting in a special way. For in the Church, while His action is always a loving, saving action, it is also always a uniting action, an action designed to restore our oneness in Christ and, therefore, our oneness in each other. The unique thing about the Church is that it is bound together into one Body by the the power and the person of the Holy Spirit. It is the people of God whom God saw fit to bind together at Pentecost into one family. The very essence of the Church is its oneness in Christ by the power of the Holy Spirit.

Nothing like this can be said about any other institution or association, yet it is the rare member of the Body of Christ who has actually found himself with abundance of meaning and quite fully identified himself as a member of this Body. If people are to be nurtured within the Holy Fellowship, and if some people are to be trained so they may be the means of nurturing others, then the first step for each is that his own orientation in the Body of Christ may be clarified and deepened and permitted to take fire.

What kind of training operation will make possible this orientation function? The Episcopal Church has used two training instruments more than any other. They are what have come to be known as "lab training" and Parish Life Conferences.

Laboratory training, or Laboratories on the Church and Group Life, first emerged in the work of the Church within the Episcopal Church, although this new training was greatly influenced by earlier developments in the social sciences. As a part of the disciplines of individual and social psychology, a new subscience known as "group dynamics" had been developing for some fifteen to twenty years prior to 1953, when the first lab in the Episcopal Church was held. Group dynamics is a discipline pertaining to the study of small groups. It is not, as many people believe, a bundle of tricks and techniques for getting people to do things, but rather the careful study of what actually happens when small groups of people come together for some purpose. Any group which is goal-seeking or problem-solving in nature would be a fit subject for observation within this discipline. Committees, both ad hoc and permanent, official boards, social groups, youth clubs, collective bargaining groups, juries, school classes, are among the many examples that qualify.

The objective of group dynamics is to observe the forces and factors affecting the quality and productivity of group life and to experiment with procedures for influencing them. In attempting to influence these forces within small groups, it has been inevitable that a variety of relatively new methods and techniques have emerged which have achieved a fairly high degree of popularity; but it cannot be stressed too strongly that the first purpose of group dynamics is observation and the development of sensitivity to forces in group life that we otherwise fail to perceive. The forces and factors of greatest interest to the social scientists in this field are the forces that bring to pass cohesiveness and those that disintegrate and divide a group into factions and cliques.

Here, then, is the first reason for the Church expressing

interest in the findings of this new emerging social science. The Church *is* a body. And the sense of belonging to a body, the members of which are very much a part of the whole, closely bound to one another in their Lord, although not an experience which can be said to be exactly common, is one that is supposed to be of the essence of the Church.

It comes as a surprise to some people to learn that group dynamics has little relation to the discussion-group movement which characterized education in the 1920's and 1930's. The only relationship between the two is that both movements deal with groups and share a certain concern about the involvement of individuals in group life. Beyond this they are as different as peas and peanuts.

Group dynamics is not only the study of small-group life; it is also the fruit of this study. The findings have taken form as a body of theory and a methodology for influencing change in group life. Both emerged from the objective observations (begun in the early thirties) of the social scientist Kurt Lewin working in a field of experience in which, previously, most of us were satisfied with untested notions. The most valuable observations of Lewin and his associates related to the needs to be found in groups, the functional roles group members take to meet these needs, and the relationship these roles have to the leadership function of the group experience. It is because of our blindness to the real nature of group needs or our refusal or inability to fill the necessary functional roles that our life in community is often essentially nonproductive, hectic, and divisive.

The fact that these observations and theories come from the social sciences, where naturalism is prevalent and supernaturalism anathema, should not deter any churchman from taking interest. No reputable scholar and no Christian with any humility would ever claim that God reveals His truth and His power only through the Church. Fact is fact regardless of who observes it, and there is much about the nature and behavior of man that requires more objective observation than the average man can be expected to provide. The Church, as well as everyone outside the Church, is dependent not only on revelation but also upon trained observation and interpretation for an understanding of man and his situation. We would do well, therefore, to keep ourselves aware of the findings of all the sciences that pertain to the study of man—anthropology, psychology, sociology, and social relations.

But the Church has particular reason to be concerned about truth that pertains to groups, and this more than anything else explains the enthusiasm and zeal with which the Department of Christian Education became involved in laboratory training. It promised to give us new awareness of the real situation in our group life in the Church.

Lab training consists essentially of three different kinds of activities: direct experience, didactic learning, and the practice of skills. In proper proportion, these elements constitute a fairly full educational experience. The first occurs in what is usually called a training group, or T-group, which meets for two hours one or two times a day over the period of the entire lab, which may run from six to twelve days. This group differs from all other educational operations in that the educators in charge supply neither agenda nor what is usually recognized as leadership. There is no teacher present to tell the group what

to do next or even what to do first. The leaders who are
present, if they are present at all (and there is a new form
of lab in the process of development which conducts
training groups with no leaders present in the actual
group session) carry out two functions. They help group
members to observe what is really happening, and they
serve as a ready resource to make available understandings about group life gained from other sources. The
members of the group have the task of supplying their
own leadership in the sense of chairmanship, and they
have the rather difficult task of determining agenda. Thus
they are ideally situated to observe and recognize the
forces in the group that help or hinder it in getting on
with its task.

The center of the lab is obviously the training group,
and it may be said to provide a form of orientation training when it enables its members to become aware of the
group to which they belong and to which they are either
contributing or not.

If the training group were all that a lab contained it
would probably have limited value. Coupled with this
extraordinary kind of experience, however, are sessions
on theory and on back-home application. These sessions
give the training group direct experience of the conti-
nuity that exists between the accumulated findings of
group dynamics and the task situation at home, the one
to which the group must return and to which its learnings
must relate.

Although the theory that is offered in these labs comes
from the social sciences, it is, for the most part, not as
complex or as technical as one might expect. For example, one observation to be made about group life is

the elementary realization that any problem-solving or goal-seeking group, if it is to accomplish its purpose, has first to recognize the variety of its needs. These fall essentially into three categories: task needs, individual needs, and group-maintenance needs. Most groups exist to get a particular job done, which is their task; and to varying degrees they are under pressure to accomplish it. This pressure constitutes one force that to some degree is always present.

Moreover, the individuals who comprise the group have their own individual manifestations of need, relating to their own schedule, their own personal life, their health, their comfort, not to mention some manifestations which are distinctly the product of their own personality. The clash of these individual needs with the task needs of the group presents a problem in communication, which in itself can create a third kind of need, namely, a group-maintenance need.

Nothing can hinder task accomplishment so much as blindness to individual need on the part of the group. And most task-oriented groups are notorious for being ill-disposed to manifest any concern for their members' individual needs. If, in addition, there is little concern evidenced for the maintenance of group morale and effective communication, the group will not be maintained sufficiently to accomplish either task or individual need. It would not be fair to imply that these three kinds of group needs and the group's response to them must be kept in balance; after all, groups move through different stages. It certainly can be said, however, that, as in the case of a stool with three legs, if any one of the three is removed or functionally impaired, the result is collapse.

There is nothing particularly new or revolutionary about this observation except that prior to the group dynamics studies there was little, if any, precise observation along these lines. And however obvious the observation may be today, the fact remains that most of us still fail to give it heed. We show little concern about the specific kinds of neglect or oversight which are affecting and limiting many of our group activities. In this sense group dynamics reveals one of its primary values, the capacity to sensitize us to that which, however simple, is still a powerful factor in our experience and one that is being essentially ignored. Barriers between ourselves and other people become barriers between ourselves and God; and when a barrier comes into being between ourselves and God, it multiplies in turn barriers between ourselves and others.

It would be possible for churchmen to analyze this simple observation about group needs as it comes to us from the social sciences and come forth with a fairly self-satisfied if not arrogant response. After all, the Christian ethic makes clear, or it should, the fact that man constantly lives in tension between the demands of the Kingdom (the task) and the need of individuals. If we sell out to either and neglect the other, we have a distorted ethic. In this is to be seen some of the tension between the personal gospel and the social gospel. At the same time the Christian, who is a child of Pentecost, lives as a member of the Body of Christ, the Holy Fellowship, to which relationship he must respond if either the needs of the individual or of the Kingdom are to be realized. In this sense the Church has a certain deep knowledge of the basic threefold tension which is the warp and woof of our existence. The difficulty has been that while we have had a theological awareness of these things, there has been little inclination to see the reflection of this tension and its breakdown in the everyday recurring experiences of our life within the Church. The social scientist has been much more observant and, in his objective fashion, free to identify forces which the Church, from a theological perspective, has always known, but usually within a context of detachment.

Laboratory training in the work of the Church has proven effective in sensitizing people to what has often been called the language of relationship, a means of communication essential for any educational program that takes engagement seriously. For engagement is relationship, the ongoing experience of God knowing man and man knowing God and not knowing God, of man knowing man and not knowing man. No design for engagement training for nurture has been as successful as this basic one for which we are indebted to social science.

Another training design which deserves to be listed under the heading "Orientation Training" is the Parish Life Conference, or PLC. In this training operation the leader asks certain basic questions for at least the first two-thirds of the conference and supplies very few, if any, answers. The focus of the questions is on the parish church and upon the conference members as churchmen. The questions, repeated over and over again in various ways and with changing depth, are: What are we doing? What are we meant to do? In attempting to answer the questions, the groups tend to move from the general to the particular in the form of role-play, and then back again to the general. But faced with being forced to stay with

these questions beyond the usual platitudinous answers
and to confront squarely the inadequacy of their answers,
the conference members are finally driven to a frustration and despair almost more than they can bear.

This PLC procedure has been criticized as one merely
providing a group of people with the opportunity of
sharing their ignorance. Seldom have so many diverse,
mutually incompatible, and inadequate explanations of
the Church been aired by any group of Christians as is
usually the case in the average PLC. In the course of
the interchange, however, the participants also scrutinize
and examine all of the answers that have come to them
through the preaching, teaching, and sacramental life of
the Church. Twelve hours of this kind of probing can
bring any average group of churchmen to the point of
literally throwing themselves on the mercy of God for
understanding and light, and in the wake of this deep
and meaningful turning to God some new understandings
about the redemptive activity of God in the Church
through the Holy Spirit can come into being.

The function of the leader is primarily to involve the
members of the group in the problem and purpose of the
conference. When light and hope begin to return to the
group, the leader is then free to share his own knowledge
and experience; but he only does so to confirm what the
conference has experienced, if this is possible. A re-
markable fact is that it is possible in an exceedingly high
percentage of cases.

In evaluating a Parish Life Conference as a device for
engagement training, it should be noted that the problem
which confronts the members of the conference is not that
they have never heard the Christian answers to the basic

questions pertaining to life in the Church, or that they are unable to verbalize these answers. The problem is that the answers they start with have had no deep and essential meaning for them and, hence, are no answers at all. Too often churchmen have never before actually been involved in a search for answers that are both objectively adequate and personally meaningful. They have not dealt with problems in a way that enabled them to be a part of the answer themselves when it emerged and, hence, to be able to understand it. There is no stronger argument for engagement training than this condition among churchmen. Both teachers and pupils are in need of a learning activity that will involve them in the very process of the religious situation they are meant to teach and to learn.

It should be emphasized that neither laboratory training nor the PLC in themselves equip people to become leaders and teachers in engagement Christian education, but they have proved to be effective ways of beginning to do so. They are only a beginning, however. Yet they are important precisely as every conversion experience in life is important, for they can open our mind to new understanding and free us to begin to work in a way which we have either never heard about or have forthrightly resisted.

Procedural Training

A second kind of training for nurture, as essential for engagement Christian education as for any other kind of pedagogy, is procedural training, procedural as pertaining to the way we do something.

There is always the threefold need: (1) to know the

essential facts of our educational operation; (2) to know the source of additional facts; and (3) to know how to use these facts. Included in the facts are not only the essential subject matter of the course but the necessary information about the people being taught. Procedural training is what has been traditionally included in the standardized leadership training courses provided both by denominational schools and councils of churches. The Church must supply resources that will enable teachers to know what ought to be carried permanently in one's memory as well as a great body of collateral material that can be used as reference.

The six volumes known as The Church's Teaching, published under the sponsorship of the Department of Christian Education, constitute the response of the Episcopal Church to this need. Anyone who attempts to teach the official curriculum of the Episcopal Church without having access to all six volumes will be seriously handicapped. It would be well, of course, if he could have read all six before teaching, yet this is not absolutely essential, since if he will make use of the many references to The Church's Teaching contained in the courses, he will not only have the information at hand which he needs, but he will actually learn it in process.

In addition to comprehending the essential facts, almost any teacher needs training in employing a methodology centered in engagement. Formal training in education for work in public and private schools does not necessarily equip a person to operate in an engagement-centered program. Indeed, it is easier, on the whole, to provide such preparation for people who have had no formal training in traditional subject-matter teaching; yet it remains true that the best of the traditional teachers will almost instinctively switch over to the use of religious issues as the organizing principle.

Procedural training must be so designed as to provide teachers with two kinds of support. In working with an essentially new methodology, the average teacher needs the group support of others who can express some of her questions and manifest some of her own confusion while she is expressing some of theirs. This group support is not needed, nor is it desirable, once the teaching begins, for as we will see later, in-service training, once the teaching begins, is greatly superior to a group approach. But prior to teaching, when a teacher is being exposed to something in principle which she has not yet experienced, much greater headway can be made in the company of one's peers who are preparing for the same task. Further, a type of training should be employed that has in it the element of practice under supervision. Those in training must be assisted to go through the actual motions of preparing lesson plans and submitting them for group criticism in the light of the standards and recommendations of the course. The Episcopal Church has used with some effectiveness a six-hour training design of this type on a Saturday, or a Sunday, afternoon and evening.

In-Service Training

Before we consider the third type of training for nurture, it should be made clear that we are not necessarily talking about a long, extensive period of training. This is not a three-year course in teacher training. The orientation training can begin on a weekend, and it is the beginning that counts. On the basis of it the teaching materials can be read, a six-hour procedural training experience can be provided, and one is ready to begin to teach, provided the third type of training is available. This third type is in-service training, a type of supervision that begins once the teaching has started. Some prefer to call it a consulting program, avoiding some of the technical connotations of the more professional word *consultation*.

It comes close to being appalling that the people who administer Christian education programs in most churches ask people without teaching experience to teach and then leave them on their own until things go so badly that the new teacher has to call for help. No one has ever suggested repealing the law that prevents beginners from driving automobiles without passing a driver's examination. We would not send our children to a dentist whose training did not go beyond reading a book on dentistry. Parents everywhere would rise up if it were revealed that their children's public school teachers had never received any formal training. Yet every year, with the best of intentions and often out of a deep desire to serve, new Sunday school teachers begin to teach with virtually no preparation and with no in-service check on what is really happening in the class.

Why do we permit this to happen? Undoubtedly there are many reasons, but certainly one of the chief is a widespread sense of frustration, sometimes resignation, in the face of what appears to be a hopeless situation. "Church school teachers are volunteers . . . They are busy . . . They can do so much and no more . . . It is hard enough to get their acceptance, almost impossible to give them adequate training. . ." Not all ministers speak in these terms, but no refrain is more common wherever the clergy gather and church school problems are discussed.

As a result of this frustration, the clergy react in various ways. Some are in favor of abolishing the Sunday church school; a few have done so. Others see no way out, but are willing to trust that something done in the Name of the Lord, no matter how little, is better than nothing. Still others, convinced that prevailing standards can be changed, have made significant progress in changing them; in these parishes teachers are being recruited who commit themselves to a program of preparation and training.

The Department of Christian Education of the Episcopal Church has tried by various means to help clergymen meet their training responsibilities in the educational field. Some clergy have been greatly assisted by the Department's proposals and training designs, but to others, the demands have only made the job harder and more frustrating. What the Church wants from the national Department is a means of improving Christian education without, at the same time, increasing the almost intolerable burden of the clergy. Can this possibly be done? The Department believes it can.

First of all, we must stop asking ourselves how we can carry on our educational mission without adequately trained teachers. We cannot. Our problem is not how to use untrained teachers, but how to train them. Our fundamental assumption must not be that the problem has no solution, but that somehow, by the grace of God, a solution will be found.

Second, we must admit that any solution, to be viable,

must be one which does not increase the demands being made on an already over-burdened clergy. There are some who may laugh at this stipulation, but they do so only by disregarding the heavy day-to-day demands made upon the average parish minister. The answer to the problem is to be found not by increasing these demands but by redistributing them.

The clergyman who looks upon his church school as that part of total parish life where children and young people are taught what they ought to know *about* our faith is not in a position to consider the church school his primary responsibility. This is important, but teaching children, under these circumstances, is not the clergyman's chief job. His principal vocation is to be priest and pastor to his people and an evangelist to the world. He therefore delegates the teaching of children to others. In fact, because his primary responsibilities are so demanding, he even has trouble allocating a significant amount of time to the training and supervision of his teaching staff. Like a doctor in the midst of an epidemic, he can minister to the sick, but has no time to develop a cure.

If, however, the clergyman once begins to think of the Sunday church school, youth work, and adult work as organized means of ministering to the religious needs of almost every child and adult in his care, then the matter of priorities changes. His principal vocation is still to be priest and pastor, but the educational program of the parish becomes one of the most productive avenues of this ministry.

This makes much sense as it applies immediately to work with young people and adults, but is it equally applicable to the Sunday church school? Actually, no more fertile field for pastoral care exists. The children are there—available, responsive, and every bit as much in need of the grace of God as any adult. The church school also contains many adults, and not alone those enrolled in classes, but teachers, observers, and supervisors. These men and women have offered themselves freely. They have much to give. Yet, at the same time, they are learners, asking for help, ripe for instruction. When the ordained minister becomes a teacher of teachers, a pastor to those who have responsibilities of leadership in the total life of the parish, he can reach out, through them, to serve the needs of all those for whom he has the "cure of souls."

The national department's earnest recommendation has been, therefore, that for a period of two months we grant to every new teacher an hour's consultation once a week with the parish minister or a qualified person appointed by him. The teacher, or the teaching team, will talk to this consultant about what happened in class the previous week and what can happen the following week—all in relation to the purpose of the course and the religious needs of the class. Eight weeks of such meetings will not turn new teachers into thoroughly competent lay ministers, but at least a new teacher will be started in the right direction. Initial misunderstandings and difficulties can be spotted and dealt with, and a pastoral relationship established as well.

Many ministers will not be able to do this with all of their new teachers immediately. But they can certainly start with two or three at a time, and, as the program moves on, gradually train some of their teachers to provide additional consulting under their guidance. Every teacher needs such support. No teacher can afford to be without it.

The major weakness of the Church's parish educational program is that it usually offers no training whatsoever for its lay leaders beyond what the ongoing life of worship and fellowship affords. The greatest weakness of training when it is offered is that it is usually confined to what we have called procedural training. As such, it is almost entirely detached from engagement. What we really need are the dynamic engagement elements of orientation training and in-service training which, when added to procedural training, constitute a training design that enables nurture to become a present reality in the life of teacher and pupil alike.

When Christian education is seen as part of the pastoral ministry, training an adequate number of teachers ceases to be a hopeless dream. We need to be certain, first, that the church school, indeed the parish itself, is firmly committed to the primary task of ministering to children and adults now, in the time of their present need of Christ; and, second, that teachers are provided, through consulting, with the pastoral support of their priest and minister. If the curriculum materials facilitate these prerequisites, the consulting sessions can become some of the most valuable hours a clergyman spends exercising his pastoral office—and the increase in the lay ministry of the Church will be tremendous.

5

Engagement Training
for Mission

In directing attention to engagement training for mission, we are entering virgin territory, for there is little explicit training for mission taking place in the Church at the present time. To the average person the very term "training for mission" suggests being trained for work in the Church's missionary enterprise abroad, or at least away from home. In the last five to ten years an increasing number of people have begun to think about the Church's mission in the world, but we have still scarcely begun to carry out the kind of training needed to equip people for that mission. If we are to do so, we need first to be sure that we see the urgency of this mission as well as its universality.

The basis and nature of our mission in the world is not to be found apart from the mission of Christ Himself.

Therefore, if any one is in Christ, he is a new creation; the old has passed away, behold, the new has come. All this is from God, who through Christ reconciled us to himself and gave us the ministry of reconciliation; that is, God was in Christ reconciling the world to himself, not counting their trespasses against them, and entrusting to us the message of reconciliation. So we are ambassadors for Christ, God making his appeal through us. (2 Cor. 5:17 ff.)

Professor Charles Price, of the Virginia Theological Seminary, has pointed out that it is the nature of the world in which we live to be diverse and to find its unity in the reconciliation of divisions. He reminds us that human life is particularly involved in a variety of differences such as economic class, nation, culture, race, the divisions of generations, and the division of sex. *Per se* these divisions are neither good nor bad. Some of them are of the created structure of the world. These divisions make human life rich and creative—and they have also become the source of destructive conflict and hostility.

The ministry of reconciliation, Christ's ministry in the world, does not remove divisions; it reconciles them, overcoming the hostility by absorbing it, while leaving the productive tension of life intact.

This activity of Christ, "reconciling the world to Himself," is of His own doing, but this same ministry of reconciliation has been given by God through Christ to the members of His body.

The Church exists on earth not so much to do something as to be the Church. Yet to be the Church the Church becomes, by the act of God through Christ, the bearer of Christ's ministry to the world. The Church necessarily, therefore, has two operating areas. One is its corporate life of listening to God and responding to God through the very nature of the corporate structure which He has provided for that purpose. The Church gathered, the Church before God in eucharistic worship, the Church

before God in holy fellowship, is the means whereby
we are carried beyond our finiteness, beyond the limitations of time, beyond even the barriers of sin into the
Kingdom, the reign of God in history. This reign became
a visible fact through Jesus Christ and remains so through
the activity of the Holy Spirit.

The nurture we receive within the Church gathered
has a twofold purpose:

1. It enables us to find our place, provided by God
   Himself, within that community in which the Holy
   Spirit lives.
2. It is also the first step in training us for carrying
   out the ministry of reconciliation in the world.

Almost all of the training now offered by parishes is
directed at nurture for life within the Church gathered.
We exhort people to carry out the ministry of reconciliation in the world. We even encourage, and sometimes
entreat them to do so. But we do not train them. We act
as though we believed that engaging in mission is a natural
consequence of being the recipient of nurture.

In this we make a mistake characteristic of our behavior in many walks of life. We like to assume that if we
do one thing another will naturally follow. We are more
comfortable when we are following a single path, a
single train of thought, a single emphasis, and it is always
a comfort to us to believe that goodness leads to more
goodness. We sometimes act as though we believe that
if we do half a job the other half will naturally follow. We
do not take readily to paradox or to dialectic, and it is
not difficult to accept the notion that mission will auto-
matically follow effective nurture.

The most appropriate illustration of this is to be found in the official curriculum materials of the Episcopal Church. When the Seabury Series first began to appear in 1955, it concentrated primarily on enabling people to find their place within the redemptive life of their parish church. This was understood at the time to be a limited objective, but, believing it to be of the very core of Christian nurture, we firmly believed it to be pregnant with all kinds of possibilities for expansion into other areas of Christian commitment. There was no disinclination on the part of the curriculum builders to deal with social issues. Some of us, indeed, had been more active in Christian social relations than in Christian education before undertaking the task of curriculum development. We firmly believed that nurture in the faith would lead inevitably to engagement in mission, and since one can only do so much in the limited time available for Sunday school and youth work and adult work at the parish level, we chose to concentrate through the medium of the church school upon training for nurture. Now we are convinced that we need to make explicit what was always there, but only implicitly.

The pure gospel of Christ, even when it is preached and communicated in all of its fullness, is seldom received or grasped in anything other than fragmentary form. The tragic blind spots we have in the areas of race relations, class relations, and international relations are the most blazing examples of this in the present era. The slowness with which the missionary movement has taken root and form on the American scene, particularly in the Episcopal Church, is another evidence of the fact that the full implications of the Gospel are not necessarily grasped just because the true warmth of the Holy Fellowship is known and appropriated. It is probably no exaggeration to say that at this very moment one could go into almost any parish of any size in this country and find faithful Christians who seriously doubt the wisdom of missionary work overseas because there is so much need at home.

While it is true that a Sunday school curriculum cannot do everything, this is no justification for cutting out one whole half of a dialectical process. To draw on Dr. Theodore Wedel's famous illustration, we do not build life-saving stations to provide nice comfortable quarters by the sea for those who will man the station. The life-saving station is built to fulfill a particular function bearing upon the lives of those who sail the high seas, and therefore the people who live in the station have to be trained to carry out that function. Consequently, not only the Sunday school curriculum but also the teaching program of the Episcopal Church for youth and adults will henceforth give itself directly both to nurture and to mission.

The one note that must be kept central in all training designs and approaches to training is that *mission* means joining ourselves to something that Christ is doing, not doing something on our own. As in the whole educational process, we are seeking to relate ourselves to an action of God in life. In one sense—and here we are dealing with a paradox—we do not go into society to convert it, or to change it, or to give it something better than it now has. All of these are needed, but they are needed at the hands of God, and they will never come to pass through the medium of self-righteous judgment. The Christian vocation in the world is not one of judgment. Our job is to relate ourselves to God's action, and when judgment is a part of that action, as it always is to some degree, we, too, stand under judgment along with those who may have nothing to do with the Church. We, too, are members of this society. Our mission in the world is to join in the mission of Christ, who is already in the world, to respond to it, and, in responding, to draw others to similar response. It is of the utmost importance that we improve our stance in this respect, for too often we take ourselves completely outside the Church by our judgmental ways, and we thereby soon find ourselves outside society as well.

It is, of course, true that many will still believe us to be judgmental when we ourselves are responding to the judgment of God, but for this we need not seek forgiveness, nor need we worry about it. The important thing is that in our own hearts, as we go about the mission of the Church, we be saved by God Himself from being guilty of judging the brethren.

Orientation Training

As in all training operations, the first kind of training for mission is orientation training. We need help in discovering the nature of the situation in which we live. Even those who know themselves to be unworthy members of the Christian Church, living in an unchristian generation, still need help in observing with some accuracy the real nature of the conflict. It is asking too much to expect any man by himself to understand with precision the inconsistencies of the two cultures to which he belongs. If he belonged only to one and were an emissary or spy in the midst of the other, he could perhaps control his subjectivity; but this rarely, if ever, is true of the Christian, nor should it be. While being a member of the Christian fellowship he is also a full member of the society we call the world. The Church does not ask him to withdraw from this world, since Christ Himself is at work in the world as a reconciling force, having already redeemed it with His blood. The choice of the monastic and the extreme ascetic who completely withdraws from the world need not interject itself at this point. Suffice it to say that the revelation of God's will which we have received through Christ and the Church suggests no such withdrawal as the ordinary vocation of man.

We need the help of one another, therefore, in understanding the limitations of our own membership and involvement in both cultures—the culture of the world, and the culture of the Church within the world. We need *consensus fidelium;* we need the mind of the Church to assist us in appraising our own specific situation in the several areas of our daily life.

There are four principal areas of our life within the world where we need orientation assistance. These are: occupation, the community (both immediate and world), recreation, and the family. Our recreational life often coincides with our life in the family, though not always. With that possible exception, it is as though we lived in four different worlds. The problems and experiences and conflicts we run into in our occupation are usually not those we encounter in the community or the home, nor are they the ones that trouble us or fail to trouble us in our recreation. And, of course, the problems and the situation of the world that lies beyond our immediate daily round are quite something else.

When dealing with cultural conflicts and the clash of

standards and the inconsistencies of life, it is of the utmost importance that we get down to particularities and not be content with generalities. It is highly questionable whether general orientation training alone can be very effective. We and the brethren need to be helped specifically by having our perception sharpened in relation to what is happening on our particular job, in the community of which we are citizens, in the particular recreation circles to which we give ourselves, in our own homes, and in specific areas of the world beyond our own home town. It goes without saying that this type of orientation has, by nature, to be engagement training. Our organizing principle must grow out of what is now happening in the lives of the individuals in the group or is currently taking place in the lives of others.

How can we do this? The Episcopal Church's extensive experience with Parish Life Conferences provides a cue. Whatever design we use must take seriously the following factors:

1. The over-all objective in the immediate operation must be to enable the focus to be on the people's view of their own situation, not on the leader's view of it or the Church's view or anybody else's view. They must identify their own understanding of their situation sufficiently to be open to being disturbed about it. The mutual stimulation that results when people openly discuss a situation in which all are involved provides the ferment that can give rise to dissatisfaction.

2. The leader must be willing to wait on the action of the Holy Spirit, withholding the authority of his own views until such time as the group is yearning for

assistance and ready to use it. Further, the leader
must recognize that even his own experience in
understanding the mission of the Church is inadequate as it relates to the specific situation under
consideration. He, too, stands in need of grace
and light as he, with the others, seeks orientation.
3. The time factor, in relation to waiting on the Spirit,
must be given careful consideration. The very
structure of most educational operations is the in-
vention of the devil in that it quite successfully
blocks man's apprehension of the Holy Spirit in his
midst. The usual one- or two-hour session held
once a week makes it possible for the average person to escape successfully the demands of almost
any educational situation. In the average run of
life, we only hear God when we wait upon Him.
We only come upon Him with any depth of reality
in terms of our own living when we give the time
that is required for digging deeply into the meaning
of what is happening to us. If there is any genius
to the educational structure of the Parish Life Conference it is to be seen in the fact that the conference
is centered on one problem alone, and the members
are forced to stay with that problem for some fifteen
hours, interrupted only by meals and sleep.

Every orientation conference, like every PLC, will be
tempted to run the full gamut of training for mission.
Even fragmentary understanding of the situation will
create an impatience to engage in some strategy planning
for dealing with it, and there will be those who will even
wish to go into the details of tactical encounter. But
both of these pressures must be resisted. We need more

than fragmentary understanding, and the leader of an orientation conference must keep the focus squarely on deepening our understanding of the real nature of the conflict. Indeed, one weekend orientation conference can very often lead to a recognized need for a greater understanding of the content of our faith, which should have been provided in earlier training for nurture. This recognized need can now be given attention as a direct result of the emerging conflict in the local situation. This is the beginning of the rhythm and the interplay between the Church gathered and the Church scattered.

Procedural Planning

The second type of engagement training for mission is training in strategic or procedural planning. A fairly accurate knowledge of one's situation in the world in its relation to the Gospel is but a prelude to the building of a strategy that will enable us to assist, not obstruct, the work of the Gospel in the world. The two ways we traditionally think of carrying out the Church's work in the world are: (1) through the institution of the Church as such, and (2) through individual Christians working individually. Neither of these is the central concern of this chapter. The Church as an institution must render organized service to society at the particular points where such service is needed. These services, which are usually social services, are the function of the Church until such time as they can be taken over, perhaps accomplished better, by society. The Church has a commendable record in this kind of organized institutional service to the world. It should be supported by every Christian. Yet this kind of mission is of a professional sort and does not really touch the ongoing life of the average Christian. It is more often the kind of service we pay others to perform for us and in the name of the Church.

Nor is it appropriate here to give much time to the function of the individual Christian acting individually in attempting to carry out his mission. In this kind of action is to be seen the traditional weakness of Protestant Christian ethics and of the Church's customary approach to the world. The very concept of individual response and action is heretical since it completely ignores the essential nature of the Church as the Body. The Church is just as much the Body when it is scattered as when it is gathered. Every member of the Church is an individual, and he always stands under the judgment of God as an individual. He will, therefore, be held accountable for his decisions and for his behavior. This behavior can never be fully blamed on someone else, unless his will has been completely violated. Moreover, as a member of the Body of Christ, every Christian is under obligation to work and live as a member of the Body, being dependent upon the Body, both upon its members and the Holy Spirit, for his wisdom and his power. Although he is under obligation to work within the Body, he remains free to operate either within or apart from it and is responsible for that decision. His approach to the world, however, should never be wholly and solely a personal, individual approach.

The over-all need for strategic planning in carrying out the mission of the Church in the world is illustrated by this disregard for a basic doctrine of the Church. We need a strategy we are not now employing, one that is faithful to the full nature of the Church and one that combines some realism about the nature of the world in which we live. We need a concept of the Church at work in the world within the world's power centers, and at work there as a Body, not one of individuals responsible only to the dictates of individual conscience. This does not mean that Christians do not sometimes find themselves working absolutely alone in some area of life, completely apart from other Christians; rather, it means that in such instances they work alone only in a physical sense, that they are under orders, that they belong to a higher command, that what they do even at moments of personal decision-making is a part of a larger strategy. Indeed, how can any institution possibly hope to permeate and affect the rigid structures and standards of modern society if its members are free agents without any form of organization in their activity, employing an almost anarchistic approach to the Lord's work, yet without the planning that even an anarchist would put into the job?

Every parish, therefore, needs to make provision for the work that churchmen will do as churchmen within their normal round of living. To cope with the problems of economic class, of nation, of culture, of race, and of family will require the formulation of guiding principles, but it will require more than bowing down to principles. The deep chasm that separates principles from the harsh and biting form the problem takes as we encounter it in our daily life is one that not only requires corporate planning but also stands in need of a corporate approach. Many a man never sees how a principle that he nominally accepts applies to choices he is called upon to make in his daily work; and even when he is conscious of the relationship, he is then not only subject to the sinfulness of his own nature, but he is often rendered incapable of acting because of an awful loneliness he feels when he sees himself standing alone against a world which will either laugh or mock.

We work together as groups in the Church sometimes (but not usually) to understand the Scriptures as they relate to our mission in the world. We have a relatively high sense of the corporate in our understanding of liturgical worship. Indeed, it is not high enough, for the Church is not really gathered unless you and I and all other Christians are caught up in this eucharistic giving of ourselves to the God of all creation and of our redemption. But at least we have some idea of the fundamental necessity of the corporate in the life of the Church gathered.

Why does the Church so quickly individualize itself and lose its corporateness when it turns to do its work in the world? Why is this mission not planned in detail in the parish house and prayed for in the house of worship? Why do we not meet regularly to share our failures, to learn from our mistakes, to be guided further by the gift of the Spirit? The most terrible thing about failure in the world, about sin and conviction of sin, is the almost excruciating loneliness of it. To a degree this will always be so and always should be so, for the individual can never divest himself of his own responsibility for his behavior; but our nature as the Church would reveal itself more explicitly if we grieved over one another's failures and sins, because we knew we were involved in them, because we knew, as members of the Body, we had had a share in the making of the plans which have perhaps come to naught. We don't do that, very much. When John Jones fails in his mission, we rarely have a sense of having failed ourselves in what he has done or has failed to do. John Jones has been on his own, a situation which no Christian ever should be in.

What kind of procedural planning, then, must we envision? The areas of planning, of course, will be determined by the outcome of the orientation, by a clear view of the tension situations that recur most frequently. In addition to the usual "circles" of women's groups organized alphabetically or by random selection, there could be *ad hoc* groups having to do with particular occupations, with particular kinds of problems. These could be in areas such as economics, industry, international problems, race, family. And each group would be a cell that could subdivide from time to time to deal with particular manifestations of a given problem. Every baptized Christian is a part of the Church's mission in the world. Every baptized Christian is already in the world, whether he wishes to take his baptism seriously or not. Therefore every baptized Christian ought to be a part of the Church's penetration of the particular part of the world in which he lives and works.

There can probably be no uniform approach to carrying out the mission of the Church in the world, and hence there is wisdom in making a cellular approach to the planning here envisioned. The resources of any parish have to be made available to all of the planning cells, but when Christians differ about the kind of planning they should do, they should be free to subdivide into additional cells and there, guided by the Spirit, make their plans.

Were the Church to publish and expound principles

alone, we would be employing an essentially detached approach to training for mission. Nor is group discussion of principles alone any less detached. When we deal with the very stuff of our daily encounter with life, then we are entering God's domain, exposing ourselves to His action, meeting Him at work as well as at worship, in the market place as well as before the altar.

Tactical Encounter

Planning is one thing, encounter another. Once we begin to carry out our plans in the place where we work, in the community where we have civic responsibilities, or in the world that reaches beyond the immediate community, we would do well to adopt the Biblical practice of going out by twos or more. In educational jargon this is the in-service training phase of the operation. Just as teachers in the Church gathered need some kind of scheduled consulting service at least during the early weeks of their new work as teachers, so a group of people who are trying to relate themselves to God's activity in the world needs the same kind of oversight and help, for this is just as distinctly a new function for them as it is for a new teacher. One can become oversentimental and overly dramatic in comparing the work of the Church in the world to a governmental mission in foreign territory, but one can also learn much from such a comparison. The briefing and debriefing, the periodic checkups, the supervision, the marshaling of resources, the great comfort in knowing that one is not alone but a member of a strong team—can we possibly afford to go about our work having neglected all of these?

Whereas planning can take place through groups in relation to common areas of concern, the oversight of tactical encounter will probably have to be made in much smaller groups of two or three, and occasionally with individuals.

The three kinds of training for mission could, in a hypothetical parish, assume perhaps the following form, recognizing, of course, that no two parishes would set up the very same program.

1. In the course of a year there would be orientation training conferences, each one attended, hopefully, by from twenty to forty parishioners. One conference might be on occupations, another on citizenship. A third could be on recreation, a fourth on the family, and still another on the state of the world beyond home. Any of these, and particularly the conference on occupations, might well lead to one or more additional orientation conferences: for example, on specific occupations, or on specific areas of community life, or on certain definite problems in the international field. The purpose of each orientation conference would be to discover the real nature of the situation in which the conference members find themselves—the demands, the pressures, the inconsistencies.

2. These orientation conferences would then serve to determine the nature of the strategic planning conferences that might follow. Sufficient organization ought to have emerged to permit both communication and the sharing of resources among these strategic planning conferences; but it is doubt-

ful whether any closely integrated command organization is either needed or desirable.

3. By the time the strategy planning conferences are in full operation, certain leaders will have emerged, even if no more than two or three, who can be available as consultants in the opening stages of tactical encounter.

The clergyman would be responsible for spearheading the over-all organization, developing the guiding principles, and procuring any resources beyond the ability of the groups to provide. His function would be to assume the major, but not sole, responsibility for keeping the basic objectives of the program consistent with the historic and central function of the Church.

Not by Episcopalians Alone

In making plans for a program such as this it is difficult to believe that very many of us will be so provincial or so exclusively Anglican, Presbyterian, or anything else as to suppose for a moment that any one segment of the broken Body of Christ by itself can make a significant dent upon the world situation. Since members of many Christian bodies work side by side at their various occupations and face the same problems, can any of us possibly conceive of undertaking a mission such as we have envisaged without reference to these fellow Christians of other communions? Here is the area of the Church's life where we can least afford to ignore the ecumenical demands of the Gospel, and it is also the area where we can most readily respond to them.

The place to begin to exercise ecumenicity is not in the Church gathered but in the Church scattered. The baffling problems dividing the Body of Christ in its gathered state before the altar do not really exist in the Church scattered; to the extent any do exist, they emerge only as work in the field drives us back to the Church gathered. Although we Christians are divided in our Church membership, we are united as fellow citizens in the world. We already work together and play together. We are sent on foreign assignments together—by our government or by industry. Can we then ignore the opportunity and responsibility we have for planning together our mission in the world and together undertaking it? The first sign of this awareness is the promising movement toward Church reunion in the so-called Younger Churches. The Church confronting a people that is dominated by another faith or ideology must be a united Church; otherwise, the Church doesn't stand a chance of carrying out its mission. And this is as true here at home as it is elswhere in the world.

For the common man, the place to begin ecumenical activity is in the area of life and work, not faith and order. The Church should maintain constant activity in the faith and order area, particularly through its leaders, but the place for the parishes to begin to undertake ecumenical activity is at the level of the Church's mission in the world. There we have much more in common with our brethren of other creeds and communions. There we are not encumbered with detached doctrines and loyalties only death can change. Once we begin working with our brethren of other communions and become engaged in mission together, we will be of a mood and temper better to study and explore differences of faith and order.

6

Evaluation and Engagement

After we have made a firm decision to center our efforts
in Christian education upon engagement, and even after
we have developed teaching and training materials that
promise to keep engagement clearly in focus, we shall
still be tempted to settle for something less. There is
always the unwelcome element of judgment in real encounter of any kind, and so both consciously and unconsciously there will be forces operating within us to avoid
it in favor of detachment. Insofar as our own responsibility for engagement is concerned, we need to make
provision for an honest and penetrating appraisal of our
work at every significant stage of the way. As stewards of
all that has been given us by God, we have that responsibility in relation to all of life, yet we are not given to
evaluating our own work critically. Instead, we wait for
other people to weigh what we have done; and although
we receive their commendation gladly, we take a jaun-
diced view toward their criticism. Just as the self pro-
tects the self from judgment, especially from the judgment that goes with engagement, so it resists criticism
voluntarily offered.

What we need is a procedure for evaluation developed and accepted at a time of relative tranquility before the more threatening moments of appraisal are at hand.

We find little tradition for this procedure in Christian education. In fact, probably no branch of education does less with evaluation than the field of religious education. The greatly increased use of evaluative procedures in elementary, secondary, and higher education in this country has no counterpart in the field of religion. Some thirty years ago professional religious educators became involved in the process of measurement and evaluation, as the considerable amount of available literature attests, much of it being a reflection of a much more extensive preoccupation with this subject in general education. It was an interest, however, that did not survive. Books on evaluation in religious education published twenty-five to thirty years ago continue to be almost the only ones available on the subject today.

Why are we so unwilling to submit what we do in the field of Christian education to rigorous appraisal? Many factors contribute to this lack of willingness. Some are merely notions and unexamined opinions we readily espouse when we need reasons for avoiding evaluation; others, less superficial, deserve careful analysis; but all need to be identified and recognized for what they are, whether they have a significant basis or not.

One fairly common explanation for not engaging in evaluation is the frank acknowledgment that Christian education is usually an amateur undertaking in the life of the Church, and amateurs are in no position to do very much evaluating. Most teachers and leaders in the local church program of Christian education are volunteers, professionally untrained, and able to give only a limited amount of their time to any particular educational operation. The volunteer teacher will, with some enthusiasm, teach his class, but it is only with considerable difficulty that he can find the time for any significant amount of preparation. It seems obvious to conclude, therefore, that it is probably asking too much to require him to find further time for evaluation. This point of view is a part of the general lethargy to which any amateur or essentially nonprofessional undertaking can fall prey. In Christian education we are tackling a problem for which we are usually ill prepared, operating on needlessly minimal budgets, using marginal time, and in the end thankful for anything that is accomplished, and all this militating against any desire to discover what was not accomplished. So long as any local parish church permits its work in Christian education to continue in this state, there is little future for evaluation in that parish, although the rise of any degree of dissatisfaction with such a situation is in itself the beginning of the evaluative process.

This explanation, however, is no justification for the absence of adequate evaluative studies at the national denominational level. Most Christian bodies in the United States employ full-time workers in the field of Christian education who, while they may be called amateurs by their critics, are far removed from that compared with the level of experience and competence to be found in the average parish. When we add to this body of workers the ordained ministers of all of the churches, we have a considerable body of full-time workers who are being employed to carry out significant functions. The time they give to their task is not marginal, so the evaluative process ought to be a built-in feature of their program. Evaluation in Christian education can at least begin at this level.

These full-time workers, however, usually are subject either to partial or complete oversight by a board that can influence or determine how funds are to be spent. More often than not this board is composed of people whose viewpoint is that of workers at the parish level. They may or may not be amateurs themselves, but they usually share the common lay notion that evaluation and research are unproductive. To some of them *research* means only *pure research,* a study that seldom relates to any task immediately at hand. "Let's get on with the work" can easily become the slogan, which, being interpreted, means that research and evaluation only slow up the process, increase the expense, and sometimes bring the whole enterprise to a state of utter confusion. The fact that all of these things can, and usually do, occur lends real weight to this not untypical board reaction. The reaction even can be forthcoming from men who are accustomed in their own business or industry to spend great sums of money on research and development, market analysis, and even in support of pure research. When it comes to the work of the Church there can be a strange reversion to a kind of primeval culture where things are kept simple and we trust man's natural instincts without really examining the product. There are exceptions to this, of course, on the part of many board members, but these exceptions are rare.

Another deterrent is the notion that sound evaluation is expensive, which is true, for evaluation usually involves a control study of all the variables that might have significant effect upon the desired outcome, and this is always costly in time and money to do. Small sampling techniques and other developments in the social sciences have placed research and evaluation on a more manageable scale, but the social sciences have also offset this economy by broadening and deepening our understanding of the evaluative process—that is, by increasing the work to be done. Some hold the view—and there is much to be said for it—that boards of Christian education should spend one-third of their budgets on evaluation and research and no more than two-thirds on program development and field services. But to say as much candidly to a board, and to advocate research on this basis, may be enough to deter it from even entering the field of research and evaluation. No board will be as likely to react in this way, however, if it has been effectively challenged to appraise the whole subject of Christian education with a discipline as rigorous as life itself demands. The important question is whether or not evaluation can tell us something we would not otherwise know about communicating the Gospel. If it can, it would be better to spend two-thirds of our budget on research and the remaining third on developing a program that would then be squarely based on the facts as they pertain to the nature of the Gospel as received by us, as communicated by us to others, and as received by others at our hands.

A more stubborn block to any kind of decisive action in favor of evaluation is the oft-spoken response, "You can't measure Christian education or religious experience." The emphasis is upon the word *measure* but it is meant to extend to evaluation in general. The word *measure* carries with it all the connotations of physical measurement, and a case can be made for the belief that it is somewhat preposterous to expect that religious growth or change can be pictured in terms of pounds or quarts or inches or numbers. Dr. Henry S. Dyer, vice-president of the Educational Testing Service, goes so far as to say that religious experience is one of those "ineffable events beyond the reach of measurement and observation." On the other hand, Dr. Leonard A. Sibley, executive officer of Research for the Lutheran Church in America, has reminded us that even in the so-called exact physical sciences few direct measurements are possible. A thermometer, for instance, does not measure heat; it measures the expansion and contraction of a column of mercury, yet this indirect measurement provides data of far-reaching value.

Men of science as well as men of religion, however, need to think twice before they use the word *can't* in relation to evaluation or anything else. The word is without valid foundation both from the standpoint of science and from the standpoint of faith. How can we be sure that Christian education cannot be measured? If all present forms of measurement are inapplicable, how do we know that it is impossible to devise new forms for this particular kind of experience? Not until we have tried and failed a thousand times do we have any right to say it cannot be done. Even then, such an assertion, while understandable, remains dubious.

What many a person is really saying when he contends that Christian education cannot be measured is, "God is at work in Christian education and who are we to evaluate God?" This is the "ineffable" element in religious experience before which Dr. Dyer stands in awe and which caused the ancient Hebrews to desist from even mentioning the name of God. Granted that man would be most presumptuous to set himself up to measure

God's behavior, this objection nonetheless has two fallacies. There is contained in it the implication that God is at work in Christian education and is not at work in other forms of education and in other experiences of life. This assumption suggests that we are free to evaluate science and social studies but that it is improper to evaluate Christian education. The assertion, of course, is ridiculous. God is at work in the whole of life, in all of His creation. Archbishop Temple said, "It is a great mistake to suppose that God is only, or even chiefly, concerned with religion." If we do not dare to evaluate anything in which God has a role, then there is no place whatsoever for evaluation.

The other fallacy in this attitude is to be seen in the degree to which it overlooks our own role in Christian education, quite apart from God's role. What kind of a doctrine of God and doctrine of man would permit us to assume that because God is at work in a human operation, our role does not matter? Is there ever a day when we are not responsible for our use of the freedom God has granted us in our life on earth? In almost every phase of religious experience our difficulties proceed, apart from sin, in large measure from faulty or erroneous theological understandings. It is at least possible that much of our reluctance to do anything about evaluation is due to the fact that the theological implications of evaluation are not as clear to us as they should be.

The Theological Basis for Evaluation

The theological basis for engaging in evaluation can be said to be threefold: (1) the nature of God in His relation to man; (2) the nature of man; (3) the nature of truth as related to man's apprehension of truth.

The Nature of God in His Relation to Man

It is sometimes disconcerting to people to discover that Christians have many conceptions of God. Even Christians who say the same Creed have differing primary images of God. He is thought of as being predominantly transcendent or predominantly immanent in life; as being essentially a spirit or essentially a power; as being One to be adored, or One to be feared. In a very real sense, He is all these, but an image of God made up predominantly of any one characteristic can profoundly influence our attitude for or against evaluation.

One fundamental observation about God, crucial not only for the Christian's attitude toward evaluation, but for his every attitude, is that God is a God of action, not a God of quiescent being. At least, all of man's experience with God would so indicate. We know Him through what He does, not from the messages He drops from heaven or the tablets we dig up from the earth. The verb forms, for instance, in the two historic Christian Creeds are significant as they relate to the nature of God:

I believe in God . . . *Maker* of heaven and earth.

Who for us men and for our salvation *came down* from heaven.

He *suffered* and was buried.

He *descended* into hell; the third day he *rose* again . . .

He *ascended* into heaven.

The central facts about God in man's experience, as central to Christian education as they are to every other aspect of life, are:

a. God is acting now in the world, in our lives—as He has in the past and as He will in the future. This is an action of demand and promise. It is an action of demand and love. This twofold action really amounts to two parts of a single action: the setting forth of His demand upon us and His offering to us of His reconciling love. God's demand and His offering of love are never separated from each other. The basic and most important fact of our existence is that God is acting within us and within the whole of His creation.

b. In this action God waits and works for our response —while granting us the freedom to respond as we will. Bishop Stephen Bayne makes the statement in his book *Christian Living* that "responsible freedom is the secret of man's existence under God," and it is in this sense that God waits and works for our response. It is true, as we say in one of our historic prayers, that in the service of God alone is to be found perfect freedom. A critic of Christianity could respond that only by enslaving ourselves to Christ do we gain Christian freedom; and in a sense this is so, but it is also true that we are thereby freed from bondage to other demands upon our loyalty. The fact is that in this life no sane mortal is ever without responsibility for the choices he makes. God is never responsible for our choices, although He is the source of the love and the power we may or may not deign to use in making them.

c. God in the end will triumph over the consequences of all of our ill-chosen responses, but this does not render insignificant our own response. This world matters and we matter, even though ultimate value is to be found neither in the world nor in us.

So, our part in the drama, our response, demands evaluation. We cannot shirk our responsibility by hiding behind the flowing robes of an almighty God.

The Nature of Man

Another aspect of the theological basis for evaluation is to be found in the Christian doctrine of man. Here, again, as in so many other aspects of reality, we find ourselves faced with a seeming paradox. We are made in the image of God, but being both mortal and sinful, we are not God. Being mortal, we are finite and are subject to all the limitations of a time-bound, essentially earth-bound existence. We not only can be wrong, but to some degree we are always wrong. It is part of our mortality and our finiteness that we are not perfect.

Moreover we are also always to some degree wrong, not merely because of our finite limitations, but because we are sinful. Always, to some extent, we are self-seeking at the expense of others. Always, to some extent, we separate ourselves from the rightful and just demands of others, including God Himself. This sin, which is ever with us, corrupts and distorts to some extent every good motive we embrace. Therefore, since we can do nothing that is perfect, and since we are always to some degree at the mercy of ourselves, we can expect our behavior to be in need of redirection and change.

Consequently, we stand in constant need of some means of taking a measure of our imperfection. Our very nature renders inevitable this need. To refuse to submit ourselves and our work to evaluation is to put ourselves in the place of God, who alone is judge of quick and dead and in need of no judgment Himself.

The Nature and Apprehension of Truth

A further basis for evaluation which proceeds from the very nature of things becomes evident if we are able to perceive the difference between truth and man's apprehension of truth. We must attempt to distinguish between the concept of truth *as it is* and truth *as we think we see it*. Hugo Munsterberg, celebrated psychologist at Harvard some years ago, used to conduct a classic experiment in distortion in his lecture hall. In the midst of a lecture a highly agitated person would run into the hall, shouting at Professor Munsterberg and threatening him in ways that electrified the classroom. When the scene ended and the intruder was ejected, the professor would have his students write a careful record of what they had heard and seen. What actually had taken place was history (in this sense, the truth) and could not be changed, but the students' versions of what took place were greatly varied and were characterized by an amazing amount of distortion. Each person who witnessed that scene was an imperfect instrument of perception. His emotions, his past associations, and his own personal involvement in the episode became barriers to accurate reporting of what had actually taken place.

No finite mind ever actually encounters truth *per se*. Truth exists and I am exposed to it, but my mind only encounters the perception of truth which I, as a person, permit to filter through to my mind. The filtering process, as well as the coloring process, can be either conscious or unconscious, although what we are talking about here is largely unconscious. This distinction between truth *per se* and truth as we perceive it can only mean that we can never be content with our own understanding of what we have done or seen or heard.

This is entirely consistent with man's general knowledge of all aspects of the created order. Is it only a matter of sheer chance that in most areas of life we need two sources of information or data in order to be able to come up with any kind of reliable outcome? It is hardly, for instance, the result of an accident of creation or emergent evolution that man is equipped with two eyes rather than one. Neither do we have two ears in order that we may have an extra one in case we lose the first. Two eyes are necessary for an image that will hold things in proper perspective. This is the difference between a stereoscopic picture and one taken with a single camera. Today we also now know the reason for and virtue of stereophonic sound.

Similarly, in navigation we need two fixes on our position if we are to know where we are. One line of position will not do. We are as lost with only one as we are with no knowledge whatsoever, but if we can obtain a second fix, then it is possible to discover our whereabouts. The same is true in the whole range of mathematics and geometry; we need two or more facts about a problem to be able to solve it.

So it is that we need two or more "fixes" on God if we are to understand Him. This is true both anthropologically in relation to our own perceptual need and metaphysically as related to the very nature of God. God is the God of love, but He is also the God of justice. Unless we have a concept of God as both love and justice, we will most certainly go off at a tangent and acquire an understanding and image of Him which is not that of the God of our Saviour Jesus Christ. Unless we understand His way as the way of law and grace, not the one nor the other but both, we will find ourselves off on another detour which will take us further and further from reality. Indeed, many of the divisions that have taken place in Christendom down through the centuries have been occasioned by man's inclination to confine his adoration and his understanding to one of God's attributes to the exclusion of others.

Because the very nature of the truth we are trying to apprehend calls for the maintenance of a balance and tension only constant checking can provide, a theological demand for evaluation in Christian education exists. In a very real sense an understanding of the role of evaluation in Christian education depends upon an acceptance of the theological basis. Evaluation can exist apart from this theological basis, but in fact rarely does.

The Role of Evaluation

The functional role of evaluation in Christian education is not only to evaluate what has taken place but also to influence the nature of what will take place so that it lends itself to evaluation. The evaluator must first make sure that the educator knows what he is doing, and he must then make sure that the educator does it.

To insist upon this twofold function is not to say that the evaluator can tell the educator what he must do. The educator must himself determine his objectives in relation both to the human situation and to the demands of the Gospel. In a certain sense and at least to a limited degree, every educator in the work of the Church already does this. But the fact is that he usually determines his objective along lines so unspecific that he does not appear to have determined it at all. He seems only to know what he is doing in a very general way. He has not formulated and accepted short-term, relatively realizable objectives.

The educator is usually weakest when it comes to the formulation of goals. This is true at almost every level of education, whether the educator is a classroom teacher or a denominational editor. It is particularly true in the area of curriculum development. The educator either never really formulates his goal, having taken it for granted, or he gives it a form that defies all evaluation. An illustration of the latter could be the objective "to teach children about God." Immediately this kind of objective raises a number of questions. To teach them what about God? To teach them about God's actions in the past? About His action in their own lives now? Which actions, then or now? To teach them about God for what purpose? What is the end result? The answers to all of these questions have to be carefully thought out and determined and, in the case of an editor, they ought to be ascertained before experimentation with any educational unit progresses very far. In the case of a classroom teacher the goals should be pinpointed and identified before a class begins to move into any given area of experience. An evaluator has to insist upon such prior decision-making, for one who is not concerned about evaluation can very easily neglect it.

Having performed this first function, the evaluator is

then in a position to carry out the second, that of helping the educator to ascertain whether he has in fact done what he proposed to do, and to what degree. Here the evaluator may employ a fairly wide selection of procedures, although many times he will of necessity have to develop new evaluation designs and instruments.

The second function is utterly dependent upon the first, and if the function of helping the educator know what he is doing is to be carried out, the evaluator must work closely with the educator from the earliest moments of the curriculum development project through the stages of publication and utilization. To suppose that these two functions of evaluation and curriculm development can be performed by the same person or persons is to credit the educator with more powers of objectivity than most men deserve. If a board of Christian education cannot afford a full-time staff member in the area of evaluation (and a case may be made for the assertion that a board which cannot afford such cannot afford to be in the field of curriculum development), it must at least so plan the functional life of its staff that, with reference to any one project, one staff member, ordinarily carrying other responsibilities, will in this instance fill an evaluation role. This kind of shared responsibility for evaluation requires general training in evaluation for all or most staff members, a requirement which in itself has advantages. If a delegation of evaluation functions does not take place, however, then we can only expect the Church to continue its present haphazard, highly subjective practices in determining the value of what it has done.

The Object of Evaluation

Finally, the question of whether or not we are to carry on evaluation and, if we do, how long we shall continue, will be determined by our identification of precisely what it is we propose to evaluate. This, of course, is the crux of the situation, and our manner of meeting it is very often responsible for many of the reservations people have about the process of evaluation in Christian education.

It is perhaps logical to suppose that the objects of evaluation will be determined by the learning theory to which an educational program adheres. One's understanding of how learning occurs and how it becomes integrated would seem to suggest the particular points in the process wherein some kind of measurement or evaluation should take place. For instance, with reference to the learning theory enunciated in Chapter 3, an evaluator might decide to develop a series of tests to supply data concerning: (1) the degree of immediate personal encounter with whatever phase of reality is under consideration; (2) the degree to which this encounter is satisfactorily identified; (3) the accuracy with which the experience is symbolized with reference to prevailing and inherited symbols; (4) the success with which the individual relates the experience to other religious experience and to the whole body of Christian faith and experience.

But the temptation to do so can be fatal! To attempt to test or measure personal religious encounter is to tackle the "ineffable," to use Dr. Dyer's term. To attempt to do so directly is at least as difficult as the task of trying to measure heat directly. Nevertheless, in both instances it is possible to isolate, identify, and evaluate the effects of the object of our concern—provided we have arrived at a decision concerning the nature of the effects which are, in fact, a consequence of the experience under scrutiny. The first task of the evaluator and the educator, therefore, is to arrive at a decision concerning the nature of the change which should come to pass as a result of the educational activity being provided.

In Christian education these changes can normally be expected to be of four different sorts, particularly if the underlying and basic objectives of the program are at all similar to those advanced in Chapter 2.

Certainly there should be a change in factual understanding. One's over-all knowledge of the experience under scrutiny, both past and present, should have undergone some change if any kind of encounter was established either with God's mighty acts in times past or His action in the present life of the learner. A simple subject-matter test will do, and there is no need for anyone to apologize for it except when subject matter is the only factor being tested. Constructing a simple subject-matter test, however, is not necessarily a simple task. The discipline of measurement has developed a number of procedures for the construction of subject-matter tests which stand a fair chance of avoiding the snares and errors that would otherwise make most tests unreliable and invalid. This professional know-how is readily available and should be used.

The behavioral influences of the experience are a second type of measurable effect. What kind of changes in the person's manner of living could one normally expect as a result of the educational activity? What practices

might be added or changed? What evident desires could
be anticipated and hoped for? What new or deepened
interests manifesting themselves in outer actions would
have significance? Certainly if a course in freedom and
authority or grace or prayer does not influence the way
a man spends the wakeful hours of his life, if such a
course does not influence those desires and aspirations
that affect his decisions, one has some reason to question
the meaningfulness of the educational experience. To
know is not necessarily to do, so it is necessary that there
be testing in the behavioral area.

Christian educators share a concern about perceptual
and behavioral change as much as do those engaged in
general education. However, Christian education must
go beyond these two changes in order to concern itself
with distinctly Christian outcomes. There are two Christian outcomes of paramount importance that have to do
with the reality of one's experience in the Church gathered and in the Church scattered.

The first of these is the third area of concern in evaluation: the data that will shed light on the degree to which
a given individual has been increasingly caught up within,
and has found his place within, the human-divine group
we call the Body of Christ. Every educational activity
calling itself Christian must have this as a primary objective. To what extent has the person experienced the
reality of a cohesive relationship not only with his own
immediate Christian associates but with the communion
of saints down through the ages? This should be an essential area of interest and concern to the evaluator in Christian education, although not to the neglect of any of the
other three. Despite the difficulty of identifying reliable

data which can indicate change in this area, the churches should pool their professional resources in the interest of developing some relatively simplified means of obtaining such data. A procedure for doing so has been used in two doctoral theses in Christian education which employ an analysis of sociometric choices, but it remains for others to simplify this test and arrive at one which can be used at the parish level.

The fourth object of evaluation should be the fact of engagement in mission when the Church is scattered. To what extent has the educational experience enabled the individual to participate in Christ's mission in the world precisely where he is now living? This is actually a behavioral change, and theoretically belongs in the second area above, but it is rarely if ever found there, and its basic importance to the whole nature and task of the Church suggests it as an area of evaluation in itself.

These four objects of evaluation—factual understanding, behavioral change, integration within the Body of Christ, and participation in the Church's mission—properly belong to all levels of Christian education, regardless of the learner's age. The expectation and manifestation of change in each of the four will differ, sometimes radically, depending upon whether we are working with preschool children or adolescents or adults. Yet all four are necessary ingredients of an educational experience that aims to be consistent with the nature of the Christian gospel.

7

The Universality of Engagement

This book is making a claim for the centrality of engagement in the Church's educational work, and we must now examine the universality of the claim.

The basis for the claim is to be found in the nature of what the Church has to teach. The very substance of Christian learning demands encounter. William Temple stated the matter succinctly in *Nature, Man and God*, when he said, "Knowledge of God can be fully given to man only in a person, never in a doctrine." He went on to say that there is great value in formulated doctrine, but its place in the work of the Church is always secondary, not primary. Temple puts it thus, "What is offered to man's apprehension in any specific Revelation is not truth concerning God but the living God Himself." In short, the Church's educational task is to communicate knowledge of God, not only knowledge about God. The one implies engagement; the other, detachment.

We have thus far been examining this claim as it relates to the work of a local congregation, both when the Church is gathered for worship and nurture and when it is scattered in the world. The work of a local church is traditionally so identified with relating people to the living God that it is difficult to dispute the claims of engagement upon the educational program of a local parish. We are under heavy demand to make engagement a focus of operations and the organizing principle of all the parish does. The point of entry, the place where engagement becomes a possibility both at the altar and in the world, in the parish house and in one's occupation, is in the situation characterized by the religious issues we experience: that is, the issues that emerge as a result of God's action and our response or lack of response. This action is taking place all of the time in the world and in the Church, in the Church gathered and in the Church scattered. God's action at the altar is in one sense the summation of His action everywhere and for all time, and there should be subsumed in our response at the altar our response in the totality of our living elsewhere. This implies that in our work in the world, by God's grace we are *engaging* with His presence and His activity. The total program of the Christian parish, therefore, has to be focused upon the moment of engagement both at the altar and in the world.

If this engagement approach to education has validity in the life of a parish, it is difficult to see how it can fail to have the same validity, indeed urgent necessity, in every educational activity of the Church, whether parish based or not. It is to be expected that many activities may present special needs requiring particularized adaptations. Two such activities, which call for careful exploration in our time, are Church-sponsored education at the elementary and secondary school levels, and the training the Church provides for the ordained ministry.

Elementary and Secondary School Education

The extent to which an engagement-centered approach to education is applicable to elementary and secondary schools maintained by the Church depends almost entirely upon the Church's reason for operating these schools. The justifiable reasons for doing so in our day are not so numerous as they once were. There was a day when the Church had every reason for organizing and operating day schools—no one else was then providing them. History records that down through the ages the Church has been a seat of learning, and its early founding of schools and colleges in this country was part of that tradition. Today, it might be argued, the Church has only one reason for being in the school business: that it has something to offer with respect to the teaching of the so-called secular subjects which cannot be provided in a system where Church and State are separated. Most other reasons amount to a rejection of a churchman's responsibility as a citizen to support public schools.

We live in a country with a long tradition for the maintenance of public schools, schools which were at the outset, as Roman Catholics rightly point out, simply extensions of essentially Protestant church schools. Whatever their antecedents, however, they are now publicly maintained, supported, and planned. The representatives of the common citizenry are responsible for their performance.

It is highly questionable whether the Church has a right to secede from its social responsibility by organizing its own church schools because it is not satisfied with the level of performance of the public schools. To turn our backs on the public school system for this reason is to take the Church out of the world. Churchmen, together with all other citizens, have a public responsibility to make the schools better if they are unsatisfactory. It is now well known what an aroused citizenry can accomplish once it decides to change its school system, for better or for worse.

When parochial schools are organized for the purpose of maintaining a form of segregation which the law of the land now says is unconstitutional in publicly maintained institutions, religion is being used as an excuse for by-passing civil law, indeed for vitiating a cardinal obligation of the Gospel itself. Under such circumstances the very question of engagement is highly irrelevant.

However, if the Church believes in a theistic universe, that God is active in all of His creation and always has been, then there are bound to be those who are dissatisfied with a school system that deletes or minimizes all mention of God's role in the study of man and nature. The Church knows something about God's actions in history; it knows something about the ethical implications of the Gospel as they relate to civil law; it knows something about the religious aspirations of men who have known God in every generation. As a consequence, it can find itself faced with some rather demanding choices in the field of education.

These choices are really no different from those we set forth at the beginning of this book. Either God is active in history or He is not. If He is not, the Church as we know it has no right to exist. If God is active in history, then the Church has the responsibility to teach history in relation to God's action in history. Yet the truth of the matter is that most church schools of the Protestant tradition use the same history books that the public schools use. The only way in which the average church day school differs from a public school is in the offering of Sacred Studies courses and the provision of Christian worship. These two elements in the school program become a kind of cultural island, with no direct relationship to the curriculum of secular studies. The main bulk of the education offered is no different from that provided in the public schools, if it is as good.

The parochial school movement sponsored by Protestant and Episcopal churches in this country, therefore, has some soul-searching to do in these days when federal support for sectarian education is a living issue. Roman Catholics do not have any problem at this point, for they know their reason for being in the school business to be a catholic, theistic reason. Their curriculum from beginning to end is planned accordingly. Non-Romans will have to decide why they desire to have their own schools (granted that most of them do not already have them); if their reason is based on theistic grounds, they then have the problem of proceeding with consistency.

The school books used in our public schools, and in most of the Church's parish day schools, reflect the essentially nonchristian cultural value patterns of our time. Basic to any value system is the understanding man has of himself and of the source from which he derives his strength. A culture is known by its doctrine of man and its doctrine of salvation. On these two doctrines are built the structure of any civilization, and from them emerge a civilization's hierarchy of values.

School books written to be used in the teaching of history, social studies, and literature in public schools reflect answers to life's basic questions that are fundamentally different from the Christian answers. The culture of our time, and of our school books, gives us a picture of man as a person, and a basically good person, although capable of deviating from that goodness. Upon such understanding of man has been built the personalistic form of democracy which places man at the center of existence. The Christian understanding of man and of his nature not only goes beyond this but also differs from it. The Church knows man to be not just a person, which he is, but a child of God. This places man in an entirely different context and saves him from the void which is the consequence of the humanistic response that the culture of the world makes. Further, the Church knows that while man is a child of God, he is also a sinner. He is not only a child of God, made in the image of God, but he is forever putting himself in God's place. The culture of our time has essentially no understanding of man's holy source nor of his sinful nature, and our school books are written against a backdrop of this inadequate understanding of man.

As a consequence, society's understanding of man's deepest needs is either lacking or inadequate. The literature of our secular heritage would lead us to believe that what man requires to meet his deepest needs is knowledge, courage, and the will to do. The Christian Church knows these fine attributes in their fullness to be derivative of something else. What man really needs is to be saved from his state of self-worshiping separation and to be helped to respond to the God who is active all of the time in his life.

Not all Christians who agree with this analysis of the

cultural gap existing between the culture of our time and
the Church would agree that our best means of doing
something about it as churchmen is to establish church
schools. Some would contend that the public schools have
values that cannot be duplicated and that we cannot afford
to lose. Rather, our responsibility is one of supplementing
them through released- or shared-time projects. Indeed,
the National Council of Churches is working on a new
curriculum for use in released-time programs of weekday
religious education which completely reverses the historic
purpose of the released-time program. The new curriculum is designed to supplement directly the principal
courses of the public school system. Previously, weekday
religious education supplemented what was being done
on Sunday morning in the Sunday school.

Others will insist that the parish day school and the
church preparatory school are our best answer. A strong
case can be made for that position only if the philosophy
of education employed in the parochial school is consistent with the demands of the Gospel. It must be remembered always that the Church is not primarily in the
business of disseminating information. What it dissem-
inates is the Gospel, and the Gospel is always the Word.
This Word, as man encounters it, is always the product
of a relationship between God and man. Indeed, it is
more than the product; it is the activity of God in all of
history in its broadest sense. The demand under which a
church day school exists, therefore, is no different from
what is known in the nurture program of a parish. The
Church always exists for purposes of engagement whether
it is at worship, in school, or at work. As an educational
institution the Church is in the unique position of being

able to teach living subject matter, because the almighty God who was and is the dominant force in all the experience of man is the same God at work in this present-day world and in the life of each learner.

Training for the Ordained Ministry

The relevance of engagement to a theological school's philosophy of education can hardly be considered without our noting at the same time the unique structure of these schools in the Church. This structure is an example of congregationalism of a special sort, and it cuts right across denominational lines. With few exceptions theological seminaries possess a high degree of autonomy and are completely free of the kind of control and uniformity which might be imposed by a denominational board or general convention. Even in the Episcopal Church, where bishops are given canonical responsibility for the theological training of their candidates for the ministry, the seminaries are completely independent of direct control by the bishops. Each seminary has its own board of trustees, and policy-making is vested in various ways in the faculty and the board of any given seminary. Despite this autonomy, the non-Roman seminaries of our country demonstrate a uniformity in their general approach to theological education which suggests that they have found a common control of their own choosing. There are curriculum experiments taking place in a number of seminaries, and at least one theological institution is making a determined attempt to substitute a four-year course of study for the traditional three-year program; but on matters such as curriculum balance, philosophy of education, and organizing principle there is probably more uniformity than any centralized control could ever have achieved.

Despite these evidences of uniformity, however, theological education in our day in this country is in a state of at least partial ferment. If one doubts whether ferment can ever be partial and whether it is ever possible to leaven part of the loaf without leavening all of it, one need only spend some time talking with theological school faculties. The fact is that most of the faculties are not well-knit bodies that lend themselves to leavening in the whole. They are the product of a university culture where every professor lives in part in the academic community as a whole, but is much more given to making his own particular discipline his kingdom and his world. He often can have more communication and sense of oneness with other scholars in other educational institutions in his own subject-matter area than with his fellow professors in his own institution. When his own faculty tackles the problem of curriculum revision, he can, in his most liberal and grace-filled moments, open his mind to hear the pleas of other disciplines or to appraise the situation of the student, but too often he responds to a primary obligation to represent the demands of his own discipline. That discipline is rarely, if ever, founded on immediate engagement.

This relatively atomistic group structure of theological school faculties, a direct inheritance from the university, means that such ferment as exists is confined largely to certain faculty members as individuals. It rarely permeates whole faculties. There are indications, however, that certain exterior forces are helping even this to come to pass. The work of the American Association of Theological Schools, greatly assisted by generous grants from foundations, is making it possible for an increasing number of deans and professors to engage in radical exploration of their important task. The walls of isolation which have tended to prevent seminaries from examining and re-examining the nature of the theological school graduate they desire to produce are being penetrated. The day is approaching when a talented young cleric will not join the faculty of a theological school to teach a subject; instead, he will co-operate in the single task of making possible the development of a certain kind of competence for engaging in the ordained ministry. This competence is only going to be achieved if the organizing principle can shift from predetermined syllabuses to the actual needs of the students who are enrolled.

Every seminarian has, as a rule, three central needs that have to be satisfactorily met by his total seminary experience if he is to be prepared to provide leadership as an ordained minister in the Church. These needs are:

1. The need to know and to understand our Christian heritage.
2. The need to be nurtured and to grow as a person in the Christian faith.
3. The need to be trained for the carrying out of a parochial ministry.

Strangely enough, it is the first of these three needs which in large measure differentiates the task of the seminary from the function of the local parish, rather than the other two, for a parish has no less responsibility than a seminary for nurturing its people and training them for their own ministry. Seminaries have a responsibility

uniquely their own in the area of subject-matter teaching.
All Christians need to know their Christian heritage, but
seminarians in training for the ordained ministry must
know many things about this heritage which the average
layman certainly does not need to know—at least at the
outset of his lay ministry, if ever. But a knowledge of the
Christian heritage, in its totality and in detail, is a necessity for the ordained minister if he is to carry out his
function in a parish with any degree of intellectual re-
spectability. In short, the average layman needs to know
the essentials of his subject-matter heritage if he is to
begin to engage in mission in the world; the man who is
to become an ordained minister needs to know not only
the essentials in detail but all of the correlative material
that undergirds and substantiates and further enlightens
the articles of our faith.

There is little question but that seminaries have seen
clearly their responsibility for fulfilling this heritage function. Very often it is essentially all they have seen. The
ferment at work in the minds of some faculty members
these days has to do with making way for a greater fulfillment of the other two needs. Some would go so far as to
say that the other two needs are of equal importance with
the need for content; that a seminary is under the same
necessity to meet them as it is to meet the need for subject-
matter learning.

Anyone who has had any experience with theological
schools knows that the fact that a student enrolls in a
school of theology is no guarantee that the historic Christian faith has taken real and active form within his life.
Among the members of an entering class there can exist
many gradations of belief and unbelief, of faith and rebel-

lion. Even when meaningful faith exists in the life of a theological student, the very nature of the analytical process which must be the approach of a reputable theological school to our Christian inheritance can place any man's faith in a state of severe tension. The need, then, for careful and wise Christian nurture exists in the seminary no less than in the parish.

It would be decidedly unfair to suggest that seminaries are completely unresponsive to this need. Again and again pastoral problems occupy hours of time in faculty meetings. The means chosen to meet the need usually turns out to be some kind of formal or informal chaplaincy service. Most faculty members try, in varying degrees, to make themselves available as pastors to their students. Occasionally a seminary calls a full-time chaplain to be the seminary pastor with the specific job of ministering to the personal need for nurture of the students.

Whether the pastoral function is shared on an unassigned basis by the faculty members or carried out by the appointed chaplain, it is traditional for this pastoral service to be kept quite separate from the teaching of the faith in the subject-matter courses. The pastoral service is an extracurricular function of the school and is not correlated with its educational activity. The education which takes place is not related to the religious issues in the lives of those who are being educated. Except for pastoral services, which are minimal and usually on a demand basis, the educational program is an exercise in detachment rather than engagement.

Adaptations of the English tutorial system prevail in a few of our seminaries in this country, but the weekly tutorial as it is practiced here cannot, for the most part, be said to alleviate the problem we have described. The tutorial is almost exclusively a means of meeting the first of the three needs—the one of subject matter. Sometimes it is simply an additional subject-matter course. Although some tutors use the tutorial as a means of providing pastoral oversight, this is not its usual function; and in any case, it is rarely, if ever, a means of correlating the resources that can meet the first and the second needs.

The most controversial of any of the three needs is the need to be trained for the carrying out of a parish ministry. Increasingly, rather than decreasingly, those who teach in theological schools espouse the position that to train men for exercising a parish ministry is not the function of the theological school. The training, they say, has to come later. In-service training is always the best, in any case; and it is presently questioned whether any man can be trained to teach and to minister outside of the context where these functions are performed. The seminary, it is argued, is and ought to be a precious opportunity where men are free to master the subject matter of their faith. In the Episcopal Church it is the traditional purpose of the diaconate to provide a period of training after graduation from seminary, although this is more tradition than reality.

This argument against training in the seminary is becoming a reversal of an earlier trend which seemed to be giving the so-called "practical" subjects a stronger place in the curriculum. Dr. Lawrence C. Little, in his recent book *Foundations for a Philosophy of Christian Education,* attests to the previous trend and, indeed, overstates it in claiming that theological seminaries generally have raised religious education from a subordinate position and have given it a place of its own with the same status, in most instances, as departments of biblical history and literature, church history, and systematic theology. It is doubtful that Dr. Little's claim fully applies in any seminary, although he is correct about the trend—until the decade of the sixties. For whatever reason, there are more professors now talking in favor of removing from the theological school curriculum any attempt at training for the parish ministry and of placing this responsibility upon denominational headquarters and the local church, than there has been since an earlier day when this procedure was assumed without being seriously questioned.

Part of the reason for this change in thinking may be that the seminaries are presently under more criticism for failing to train their students to carry out their parish ministry than they were a few years ago when they were actually doing much less than they are now. Anyone who has any knowledge of what is happening in the parishes of our Church and the pattern that is repeated again and again when the newly ordained man begins his parish ministry cannot fail to realize that whatever is being accomplished by pastoral theology courses in seminaries, these courses are not training their students to meet the contingencies of parish life in the field of pastoral care and education. Some preparation for preaching and pastoral care is offered in all of our seminaries, but it is questionable whether this can really be called training, except where realistic practice preaching is offered and where extensive clinical pastoral training is required. Through teaching programs a very limited preparation is provided for meeting the nurture needs of a parish, but there is essentially no supervised training. And nowhere in the Church's seminaries is any supervised training being offered for the training of the laity in carrying out the mission of the Church when the Church is scattered.

There is at least some reason, therefore, to ask whether theological education has arrived at a place where it would be timely to explore the whole matter of philosophy of education as it relates to the total task of preparing people for the ministry. Can the communication of the Gospel be accomplished apart from a rigorous blending of God's mighty acts of old with His actions today in our own lives? Can people be trained in communicating the Gospel without exposing them not only to what is being communicated but also to the people who are the recipients of this communication and to the situation in which the communication will take place? Does the very nature of the Gospel itself place any demands upon us in these matters? Does the Gospel differ from all other objects of education in that it can only be apprehended via a merger of the historical and the existential? In this century, when we are acutely aware of the tremendous force of culture in contributing to the social and international unrest of our time, can seminaries possibly afford to teach their Gospel subjects apart from the study and exploration of the cultural milieu in which the seminaries are going to have to communicate the Gospel if it is to be communicated at all?

To assert that it is utterly impossible to face up to all of these issues in the course of three years, or even four years, does not justify tabling the matter. The fact is that if a normal seminary course lasted seven years, theological school professors would still not be able to include all of the things they would like to cover and which, justifiably, should be covered. The important question is whether the very nature of the Gospel we are communicating makes it mandatory for us to place engagement at the center, engagement both as it relates to the seminarian's own encounter with God and as it relates to his encounter with other people's situation in the world outside the seminary cloisters. If there is such a Gospel demand upon us, then our response must be the same whether we have one year or seven available for a training program. A faithful balance of the three needs will be sought.

Thirty years ago when Angus Dun, recently retired Bishop of Washington, was Professor of Theology at the Episcopal Theological School, Cambridge, he carried out his functions as a teacher of theology in a way that achieved a high degree of balance among the three needs. He established as a requirement of his course in systematic theology that his students visit patients at a vast state institution combining a general hospital, a tuberculosis sanitarium, and a hospital for the mentally ill. Under the supervision of, first, the social worker and later a chaplain, they visited selected patients and turned in detailed reports on their ministrations. Professor Dun read these reports and responded to them both in his lectures on theology and in personal tutorial conversations with the students. This took place in an era in theological education when professors of pastoral care, insofar as they existed, were just beginning to institute clinical training as an important adjunct of their own discipline. Angus Dun was using it as a means not only of communicating theology but also of coming to grips with the real theological questions which were in a state of ferment in the minds and souls of his students. This was something he could only make contact with at the place where it is most accessible, where the need exists to receive the Gospel, and where the Gospel is actually in the process of communication. This was engagement teaching of theology.

In the end all education in the name of the Church must decide precisely what it will put first and what second—whether to prepare people for the future or to minister to them where they are now—whether to transmit culture or develop a culture change agent—whether to generate motivation that is essentially self-dependent or motivation that is grace dependent. The fact that the Church must perform *all* of these services to varying degrees does not remove the problem of priority. Which task will be placed first is the bedrock problem in Christian education today—as it always has been.

Selected Books

Theological Foundations

Bonhoeffer, Dietrich, *The Cost of Discipleship*. New York: Macmillan Company, 1948.

Bonhoeffer, Dietrich, *Life Together*. New York: Harper & Brothers, 1954.

Brightman, Edgar S., *Persons and Value,* Boston, Mass.: Boston University Press, 1952.

Brunner, Emil, *The Divine-Human Encounter*. Philadelphia: Westminster Press, 1943.

Brunner, Emil, *The Misunderstanding of the Church*. Philadelphia: Westminster Press, 1953.

Buber, Martin, *Between Man and Man*. New York: Macmillan Company, 1948.

Buber, Martin, *I and Thou*. New York: Charles Scribner's Sons, 1937.

Butler, J. Donald, *Four Philosophies and Their Practice in Education and Religion*. New York: Harper & Brothers, 1957.

Butler, J. Donald, *Religious Education*. New York: Harper, 1962.

Kraemer, Hendrik, *A Theology of the Laity*. London: Lutterworth Press, 1958.

Kraemer, Hendrik, *The Communication of the Christian Faith*. Philadelphia: Westminster Press, 1956.

Miller, Allen, *Invitation to Theology: Resources for Christian Nurture and Discipline*. Philadelphia: Christian Education Press, 1958.

Miller, Donald G., *The Nature and Mission of the Church*. Richmond, Virginia: John Knox Press, 1957.

Niebuhr, Reinhold, *Moral Man and Immoral Society*. New York: Charles Scribner's Sons, 1932.

Niebuhr, Reinhold, *The Nature and Destiny of Man*. 2 vv. New York: Charles Scribner's Sons, 1941, 1943.

Pike, James A., and Pittenger, W. Norman, *The Faith of the Church*. Greenwich, Conn.: Seabury Press, 1951.

Pittenger, W. Norman, *Rethinking the Christian Message*. Greenwich, Conn.: Seabury Press, 1956.

Pittenger, W. Norman, *Theology and Reality*. Greenwich, Conn.: Seabury Press, 1955.

Religious Education Association, *What Is the Nature of Man: Images of Man in Our American Culture*. Philadelphia: Christian Education Press, 1959.

Shinn, Roger L., *The Existentialist Posture*. New York: Association Press, 1959.

Temple, William, *Nature, Man and God*. London: Macmillan and Company, 1934.

Thomas, Owen C., *William Temple's Philosophy of Religion*. London: SPCK; Greenwich: Seabury Press, 1961.

Tillich, Paul, *The Courage to Be*. New Haven, Conn.: Yale University Press, 1952.

Tillich, Paul, *Systematic Theology*. Chicago: University of Chicago Press, 1952.

Tillich, Paul, *Theology of Culture*. New York: Oxford University Press, 1959.

Wolf, William J., *Man's Knowledge of God*. Garden City, New York: Doubleday & Co., 1955.

Wright, G. Ernest, *God Who Acts: Biblical Theology as Recital*. Chicago: Henry A. Regnery Company, 1952.

Philosophy and Methodology of Christian Education

Chaplin, Dora P., *The Privilege of Teaching*. New York: Morehouse-Barlow Company, 1962.

Cully, Iris V., *The Dynamics of Christian Education*. Philadelphia: Westminster Press, 1958.

Howe, Reuel, *The Miracle of Dialogue*. Greenwich: Seabury Press, 1963.

Ligon, Ernest M., *A Greater Generation*. New York: Macmillan Company, 1948.

Little, Lawrence C., *Foundations for a Philosophy of Chris-*

tian Education. Nashville, Tennessee: Abingdon, 1962.

McCluskey, Neil G., *Catholic Viewpoint on Education.* Garden City, New York: Hanover House, 1959.

Miller Randolph C., *Biblical Theology and Christian Education.* New York: Charles Scribner's Sons, 1956.

Miller, Randolph C., *The Clue to Christian Education.* New York: Charles Scribner's Sons, 1950.

Miller, Randolph C., *Christian Nurture and the Church.* New York: Charles Scribner's Sons, 1961.

Miller, Randolph C., *Education for Christian Living.* Englewood Cliffs, New Jersey: Prentice-Hall, 1956.

Murray, A. Victor, *Education into Religion.* New York: Harper & Brothers, 1954.

National Council of the Churches of Christ in the U.S.A., Division of Christian Education. *A Guide for the Curriculum in Christian Education.* Chicago, 1955.

Sherrill, Lewis J., *The Gift of Power.* New York: Macmillan Company, 1955.

Sherrill, Lewis J., *The Rise of Christian Education.* New York: Macmillan Company, 1944.

Sherrill, Lewis J., *The Struggle of the Soul.* New York: Macmillan Company, 1951.

Smart, James D., *The Teaching Ministry of the Church.* Philadelphia: Westminster Press, 1954.

Smith, H. Shelton, *Faith and Nurture.* New York: Charles Scribner's Sons, 1941.

Vieth, Paul H., *The Church School.* Philadelphia: Westminster Press, 1957.

Vieth, Paul H., *Objectives in Religious Education.* New York: Harper & Brothers, 1930.

Wyckoff, D. Campbell, *The Gospel and Christian Education.* Philadelphia: Westminster Press, 1959.

Wyckoff, D. Campbell, *The Task of Christian Education.* Philadelphia: Westminster Press, 1955.

Wyckoff, D. Campbell, *Theory and Design in Christian Education Curriculum.* Philadelphia: Westminster, 1961.

Wyckoff, D. Campbell, *How to Evaluate Your Christian Education Program*. Philadelphia: Westminster, 1962.

Training for Nurture and Mission

Bayne, Stephen F., Jr., *Christian Living*. Greenwich, Conn.: Seabury Press, 1957.

Bushnell, Horace, *Christian Nurture*. New Haven: Yale University Press, 1947.

Dillistone, F. W., *Christianity and Communication*. New York: Charles Scribner's Sons, 1956.

Howe, Reuel L., *The Creative Years*. Greenwich, Conn.: Seabury Press, 1959.

Howe, Reuel L., *Man's Need and God's Action*. Greenwich, Conn.: Seabury Press, 1953.

Kean, Charles D., *The Christian Gospel and the Parish Church*. Greenwich, Conn.: Seabury Press, 1953.

Little, Sara, *The Role of the Bible in Contemporary Christian Education*. Richmond: John Knox Press, 1961.

Miles, Matthew B., *Learning to Work in Groups*. New York: Bureau of Publications, Teachers College, Columbia University, 1959.

Moreau, Jules L., *Language and Religious Language*. Philadelphia: Westminster Press, 1960.

Muelder, Walter G., *Foundations of the Responsible Society: A Comprehensive Survey of Christian Social Ethics*. Nashville, Tenn.: Abingdon Press, 1959.

Musselman, G. Paul, *The Church on the Urban Frontier*. Greenwich, Conn.: Seabury Press, 1960.

Southcott, Ernest W., *The Parish Comes Alive*. New York: Morehouse-Barlow Company, 1956.

Spike, Robert W., *In But Not of the World*. New York: Association Press, 1957.

Whittemore, Lewis B., *The Church and Secular Education*. Greenwich, Conn.: Seabury Press, 1960.

Winter, Gibson, *The Suburban Captivity of the Churches*. Garden City: Doubleday and Company, 1961.